THE D🐾G BEHAVIOR
answer book

The DOG

BEHAVIOR

answer book

**Understanding and Communicating
with Your Dog to Build a Strong,
Happy Relationship**

2nd Edition
**COMPLETELY
REVISED &
UPDATED**

ARDEN MOORE

Storey Publishing

The mission of Storey Publishing is to serve our customers by publishing practical information that encourages personal independence in harmony with the environment.

Edited by Deborah Burns and Lisa H. Hiley
Art direction and book design by Erin Dawson
Text production by Liseann Karandisecky
Indexed by Christine R. Lindemer, Boston Road Communications

Cover photography by © annaav/stock.adobe.com, front, t.c.; Courtesy of Atali Samuel Photography, front, b.l.; © BilevichOlga/stock.adobe.com, front, t.l.; © carebott/Getty Images, back; © Kate Lacey, front, b.c. & b.r.; © smrm1977/stock.adobe.com, front, t.r.
Interior photography credits appear on page 217

Storey books are available at special discounts when purchased in bulk for premiums and sales promotions as well as for fund-raising or educational use. Special editions or book excerpts can also be created to specification. For details, please call 800-827-8673, or send an email to sales@storey.com.

Storey Publishing
210 MASS MoCA Way
North Adams, MA 01247
storey.com

Library of Congress Cataloging-in-Publication Data on file

Printed in the United States by Versa Press
10 9 8 7 6 5 4 3 2 1

I dedicate this book to all the dogs in my life, past and present, who have made me a better person. Special paws up to Pet Safety Dog Kona, who assists me in my pet first aid and pet behavior classes and loves visiting seniors and kids as a certified therapy dog.

A big tail wag to my pet-loving family, especially Julie, Deb, Karen, Kevin, Jill, Rick, Laura, Chris, Susie, Jim, and Geoff. And I thank Janice Dean, my high school journalism teacher, for her support and encouragement throughout my writing career.

CONTENTS

113
Righting Doggy Wrongs

Life with an undisciplined dog is no fun for anyone, including the dog. Explore the importance of good training, learn about common behavioral issues, and discover how to raise a mannerly pup or teach an old dog some new tricks.

145
Achieving Health and Harmony at Home and Away

We love our dogs, but sometimes they drive us crazy. And sometimes it's hard to tell who's the top dog in the family. Figure out ways to exist more peacefully with your best friend, and learn about taking your dog with you to all kinds of places.

187
Changing Lives, Parting Ways

Life is full of changes and choices, some of them difficult. Our pets are affected by everything we do. Here are some tips for coping with death, divorce, moving, and more.

PREFACE

If only our dogs could get by on their cute looks. But if they don't learn good doggy manners and have consistent training, some dogs grow up to be more challenging than cute. More fearful than fun. More bossy than benign.

It may take months, weeks, or just days for the people/pet honeymoon to end and the problem-solving phase to begin, but most dog owners wind up with at least a few questions or concerns about their canine companion. You don't know why your dog bark-bark-barks when you conduct a Zoom call. You get embarrassed when your dog greets your date by sniffing his butt. You are puzzled as to why your dog just will not quit chasing that tennis ball, even when you're totally tired of tossing it.

> **Once people find out what I do for a living, they unleash their questions.**

You are looking for answers. You are looking for ways to bolster your connection with your canine. You've come to the right place. Since I authored the original *The Dog Behavior Answer Book* in 2006, so much has changed in the dog world as well as in our lives. Think about it. Back then, Facebook was in its infancy. Hardly anyone drove electric cars. Netflix was still mailing out DVDs, not streaming its own content.

A lot has changed in the dog world, too, and mostly for the better. People are more inclined to call themselves pet parents than pet owners. Well-mannered dogs are welcomed at more and more pet-friendly cafés, hotels, and vacation rentals. Dogs have access to better food, more sophisticated medical treatment, and more sports such as dock diving and scent work.

Annual pet trade shows like Global Pet Expo can fill convention centers with exhibitor booths stretching the length of seven football fields. Dogs have become powerful social influencers on Instagram, Facebook, and TikTok. There is even a cable channel dedicated to home-alone dogs called DOGTV.

For these reasons and many more, I knew it was time for a major update to my original book. Since 2006, I've added to my canine knowledge by learning from top veterinarians and dog behaviorists. I am a certified pet professional and national speaker for Fear Free Pets, a global group dedicated to teaching pet professionals and pet parents about ways to alleviate fear, anxiety, and stress in our dogs at home, at the veterinary clinic, on the road, and in new situations.

I became a master certified pet first aid/ CPR instructor and conduct classes with Pet Safety Dog Kona. I am a regular columnist for *Dogster* magazine, and I frequently speak to professional pet sitters, doggy day care staffs, and animal shelters. My weekly podcast, *Oh Behave*, launched in 2007 on Pet Life Radio and is now the longest continuously running pet podcast, with more than 500,000 loyal listeners all over the globe. I love learning and sharing great insights about pets from top experts.

Once people find out what I do for a living, they unleash their questions. *Why does my dog…? How can I get my dog to stop…? What is the best way to teach my dog to…?* So, I invite you to paw through these pages. You might nod in agreement as you read these questions from other dog lovers and then sense the light bulb click inside you as I offer practical solutions.

Got dog? Count yourself doggone lucky. I know I do.

Paws up!

Arden Moore

What It's Like to
BE A DOG

Put yourself in your dog's paws for a moment. Ancient dogs roamed in packs to hunt for food. They had—and modern dogs still have—a respect for social ranking. Then about 15,000 years ago, dogs and humans developed a relationship unparalleled in history. In exchange for food and shelter, dogs agreed to help humans in countless ways, becoming our partners, coworkers, and pals.

Realizing that dogs possess many desirable traits, people have manipulated canine genes to produce dogs made to hunt, herd, guard, and simply snuggle. The American Kennel Club recognizes more than 200 breeds in all sizes and shapes, and there are many others all over the world. Some of these dogs weigh more than 150 pounds; others can literally fit in the palm of your hand.

The quest to create the perfect dog from blended breeds—dogs who don't shed, have loving temperaments, and are easy to train—has produced oodles of hybrids, such as labradoodles (Labrador retriever/poodle), puggles (pug/beagle), and poochins (poodle/Japanese chin). Millions more with unknown lineage fall into the almighty mutt category.

With all these breeds and mixes come many different looks. Ears can be floppy, pointy, cupped, folded, or erect. Muzzles range from long and narrow to smushed flat. Canine coats can be wiry, curly, fluffy, double-coated, or flat. The komondor even has dangling dreadlocks! And dogs come in all kinds of colors and patterns, including spots and stripes.

Yes, dogs put a capital D in diversity. And they unleash a big D for devotion to their favorite humans. In spite of all our meddling through the years, the true nature of dogs never wavers: They love us just the way we are.

NOW EAR THIS, HOO-MAN!

My Siberian husky can be snoozing upstairs in the back bedroom, but within seconds of me opening a bag of potato chips in the kitchen, she appears, tail wagging and ready to share. When we go out on walks, I am amazed at how she turns her head at things I don't hear, like a rustling squirrel or chirping bird. I always thought I could hear well, but can my husky outhear me?

Ear-ye! Ear-ye! When it comes to hearing, dogs have us beat, paws down, so don't challenge your husky to a listening contest. Canine hearing is about two times better than that of humans. Dogs can hear sounds four times farther away, which explains why your husky hears small sounds that you don't catch.

Canine ears, whether erect like your husky's, bat-shaped like a French bulldog's, droopy like a bloodhound's, or folded like beagle's, capture more sounds at greater distances and wider frequencies than human ears. Even breeds like cocker spaniels with thick, floppy ears can distinguish the sound of their owner's car from all other traffic a block or more away. Their talented ears can zero in on sounds even in a noisy environment.

Dogs have about 18 muscles in each ear. In addition to their keen hearing, dogs use their ears to maintain their equilibrium while moving. More

Can You Hear Me?

Hertz (Hz) is a measure of sound frequency, or cycles per second. People can hear sounds in a frequency range between 63 and 23,000 Hz. Dogs can hear in ranges between 67 and 45,000 Hz, but they take a back seat to the family cat in hearing abilities. Cats can capture sounds between 45 and 64,000 Hz, making them much better at tuning in to a mouse in the house. But neither owns bragging rights to having the best hearing on the planet. That belongs to moths! Dogs rank sixth in hearing behind moths, bats, owls, elephants, and cats.

importantly, dogs also use their ears to express their emotions. Ready-for-play dogs often arch their ears up and forward and may even cock their heads to one side. Confident dogs raise their ears forward while giving a steady, nonthreatening stare. Curious dogs may cup their ears to zero in on that one-dimensional animal on your TV screen that they can see but not smell. Many dogs flatten their ears against their heads when they are scared or about to get in a fight. 🐾

THE WINNER BY A NOSE

On our daily walks, I'm puzzled as to why Sally, my hound mix, will stop abruptly to intently sniff a fire hydrant or the base of a telephone pole. What is she smelling that I can't? How does my sense of smell compare to hers?

The phrase *led by the nose* takes on a whole new meaning in the canine world. Olfactory receptor cells inside the canine nose are bolstered by tiny hairs called cilia that are coated with mucus to help trap scents. People have about 5 million olfactory receptor cells, compared with more than 100 million in dogs.

And some breeds have even more refined scenting skills. Bloodhounds reign as the scenting champs with about 300 million of these cells, compared to a dachshund, with 125 million. Beagles, Labrador retrievers, and German shepherds also rank high in detecting scents.

These receptors are capable of breaking down the individual ingredients in each scent. So not only can your dog tell if you're baking a chicken or a turkey, she can also distinguish the particular spices you put in the stuffing.

If someone dropped a potato chip in a swimming pool, your dog's mighty nose could easily detect it.

During neighborhood walks, Bujeau, our Bernese mountain dog mix, meanders nicely on a leash until her nose kicks into gear and she stops to guide her nose up and down and all around a fire hydrant. Sometimes she plops right down into the grass to get a better sniff of something I don't see and definitely don't smell.

Sally and Bujeau are performing doggy downloads. When dogs sniff a telephone pole or a fire hydrant, they are gathering lots of facts about previous dogs who urinated on these objects. Call it pee mail. They don't need computers or smartphones to gather up a lot of data about the pee-depositor, who may now be blocks away snoozing on the

13

sofa at home. With their superior sense of smell, they can even detect the type of paint used on fire hydrants.

The canine nose really gets put to use in meet-and-greets. We shake hands; dogs sniff each other's rear ends. It is a quick, dependable way to learn about the other dog's emotional state, health status, gender (even those spayed and neutered), and, to some degree, most recent meal.

Bottom line: Your dog can smell about 10,000 times better than you can (although he probably smells worse before bath time)! 🐾

Sniff It Out!

Dogs possess about 20 times more scent-receptor cells than humans. They can use their noses to sniff out odors that contain only a few parts per billion.

SEEING EYE TO EYE

Our dog Ginger pays attention to everything on the television screen, especially if there is a nature program that shows wildlife, particularly squirrels. But our other dog, Rambo, doesn't pay any attention to anything on TV. Why the difference, and how do dogs use their vision compared to us?

Veterinarians and animal behaviorists are still exploring the reasons why some dogs fall into the "mutt-see" TV group and others do not. Gone are the days of analog televisions relying on rabbit ear antennae and producing fuzzy, sometimes flickering images. Today, high-definition televisions can fill entire walls, making images sharper and more realistic.

Dogs are more likely to respond to these one-dimensional birds and squirrels even though they do not emit any odors. In response to this growing canine audience comes DOGTV, a cable channel dedicated to entertaining and engaging home-alone dogs. Launched in 2012, it airs in more than 120 million households in 15 countries.

But let's put down that TV remote and discuss how we see eye to eye with our dogs. It turns out we have more in common visually with them than we do in the categories of hearing and smelling, where dogs beat us, paws down. We rely more on our vision than dogs do, and we do see a wider range of more vivid colors. That's because dogs see the world with dichromatic vision. Nix the notion that dogs can only see in black and white and shades of gray. They do see some colors, primarily blue and yellow, but not as many as we can. With our trichromatic vision, we see a full rainbow of colors.

And dogs don't wear glasses, but they are more nearsighted than humans. Studies confirm that dogs have 20/75 vision, which means an object that a dog could identify at 20 feet, we could detect from 75 feet away.

However, canine eyes win points when it comes to detecting movement. Dogs also can see better in dim light than humans because of a reflective layer of cells located beneath their retinas called the tapetum lucidum. Dogs are blessed with better peripheral vision, too. Standing still, dogs can see up to 250 degrees without turning their heads, while people can see, at best, up to 180 degrees.

Combined, these canine traits explain why your dog can spot a bird flying by at dusk sooner—and better—than you can. However our vision stacks up, there's no question that those big brown puppy eyes are hard to resist when your dog wants a treat! 🐾

BRAINY BREEDS

Certain dog breeds seem to be smarter than others, so I purposely chose a border collie in part because of the breed's reputation for brains. I didn't want to fuss with a less-intelligent breed when it came to teaching basic obedience. I don't have the patience to keep trying and trying to teach a dog to sit or to stay. So far, I've been really happy with Einstein's response to training, but I'm curious: How can I figure out just how smart he is?

In the canine classroom, your aptly named Einstein rates as the tail-wagging valedictorian. Other top students include poodles, German shepherds, and golden retrievers. Breeds that might need some after-school tutoring include Afghan hounds, basenjis, and bulldogs. Before owners of these dogs bark back in protest, please keep in mind that exceptions—both bright and not so bright—exist in every breed.

Sizing up a dog's brainpower can be tricky, because dogs don't think the way we do. They are not begging to enroll in the canine version of Mensa or paw-swiping your tablet to do online sudoku. Because certain breeds were created to excel at certain tasks, your

border collie can run circles around a Japanese chin when it comes to herding sheep because he possesses the genes to shepherd a flock. But I'd put my money on a beagle sniffing out a rabbit faster than a border collie, since following their noses is a bragging right among hound breeds.

But almost any dog can learn a wide variety of obedience cues if taught with patience, and many can acquire an astonishing array of behaviors. Service dogs are an amazing example of the canine brain in action. These special dogs are encouraged to exercise "intelligent disobedience" when confronting a situation that could harm their human charges. A Seeing Eye guide dog, for example, knows not to budge forward when facing a hole or other hazard, despite his handler's insistence.

Developing a foolproof method of testing dog smarts remains an ongoing challenge for dog trainers, breeders, and animal behaviorists. One pioneer in this field is Stanley Coren, a renowned psychologist and exceptional dog trainer. In *The Intelligence of Dogs*, Dr. Coren ranks 133 breeds from smart as a whip to dumb as a brick, pointing out there are variations and exceptions in every breed. He devised a canine IQ test that strives to identify several levels of intelligence: adaptive, obedient, and instinctive.

Breeds ranking in the top 10 smartest can grasp new commands in fewer than five repetitions and obey a known cue the first time it is given 95 percent of the time. Your border collie heads this elite class and is joined by poodles, German shepherds, golden retrievers, Doberman pinschers, Shetland sheepdogs, Labrador retrievers, papillons, Rottweilers, and Australian cattle dogs.

Breeds in the bottom 10 often require up to 100 repetitions to absorb a new command and will obey a known cue the first time it is given only 25 percent of the time. Even if they know how to sit, they may need to hear the word four or five times before they plop their rear end down. This list, which is definitely subject to debate, includes the basset hound, mastiff, beagle, Pekingese, bloodhound, borzoi, chow chow, bulldog, basenji, and Afghan hound.

Of course, if you asked the dogs, the "dunces" might reply that they are plenty smart but they just choose to ignore those commands! 🐾

Breed Byte

Silence is golden for the basenji, an African dog that does not bark. Basenjis do vocalize, however, with distinctive yodels, yowls, and whines.

How Smart Is Your Dog?

Here are a few fun ways to gauge canine smarts.

The Towel Test. When your dog is lying down, drape a large bath towel over his head and time how long it takes for him to lose the towel. Smart dogs master this in less than 15 seconds while slow learners can take more than 30 seconds.

The Bucket Test. Line up three containers upside down on the floor (size is not important, but use lightweight ones like yogurt tubs—thoroughly washed, of course!). Show your dog his favorite treat or toy and let him watch you place it under one of the containers. Divert his attention away from the buckets for a few seconds and then ask him to find the hidden prize. A smart dog will make a beeline to the correct bucket while a slower learner may knock over the other two containers before finally finding the prize.

The Leash Test. Pick a time that you do not customarily walk your dog—say midmorning or midafternoon. Without saying anything, pick up the leash and your house keys in full view of your dog. A smart dog associates the leash and keys with a walk and becomes excited at the prospect of going out. A not-quite-so-bright dog won't make the connection and may need to hear "Want to go for a walk?" before jumping for joy. (Of course, a more phlegmatic dog may just not be in the mood for a walk!)

Remember that canine IQ tests have limitations, one of which is that the results are subjective and evaluated by people, not other dogs. So a dog who may seem dumb to us could be the leader of the pack in the eyes of other dogs. Whatever the test results, the important thing is to value the love your dog gives you more than the number of brain cells he maximizes.

DON'T JUDGE A DOG BY HER BREED

I am a bone-a-fide Labrador retriever fan. I love, love, love this breed, and I love throwing balls for my dogs to fetch. However, my newest Labrador retriever, whom I adopted from a breed rescue group, has absolutely no interest in retrieving balls. Sage is about 1 year old. She is super smart, super sweet, and walks nicely on a leash. She will engage with me in a friendly game of tug but gives me a blank look and doesn't budge when I toss a tennis ball in our backyard. Why is that?

With the word *retriever* in the breed name, it's easy to see why you have a small case of canine confusion. The American Kennel Club recognizes nearly 200 breeds, grouping them into categories based on certain traits. These groups are sporting, hound, working, terrier, toy, nonsporting, and herding. Sage falls into the sporting group of breeds that were developed to capture and bring back feathered game, often from a pond or lake. But there are exceptions to every rule, and even though people have purposely bred dogs for centuries to produce certain desired traits, there is no 100 percent guarantee that every dog will perform according to the genetic tweaking of its breed.

My friend Flo loved her miniature schnauzer, whom she dubbed "Barky Buddy" because he would unleash loud, high-pitched yelps and fling himself against the front door screen anytime an uninvited solicitor tried to talk to Flo about adding new siding or switching cable companies. Buddy's loud barks prevented the salesperson from giving his pitch, and as a result the person would make a quick apology and leave.

After Buddy passed away, Flo adopted a pair of miniature schnauzers named Twyla and Tiny. Guess what? Despite being full-blooded members of the terrier group with reputations for being vocal and a bit stubborn, Twyla and Tiny are very quiet. They rarely bark. They stay on the sofa when the doorbell rings, forcing Flo to answer sans schnauzers.

Sage is a wonderful Labrador, with many of the breed's cherished traits, including a friendly and outgoing temperament. But ball fetching just isn't her thing. I suggest you look for something else that you can enjoy doing together. She may want to use her nose to find hidden objects indoors and outdoors in the fast-growing sport of scent work, also known as nose work. If you like water sports, see if she has the sea legs to join you on a paddleboard or even in a kayak or a small boat. Or she may flourish as a certified therapy dog and bring smiles to kids in schools or people in hospitals. Consider yourself lucky—you definitely have one special Labrador retriever. 🐾

TRUE PUPPY LOVE

I adore my dog and would do anything to keep her safe and happy. I love to spoil her with new toys and take her with me in the car. I know that I truly love her, and I think she loves me, too. She wags her tail at me, gives me sloppy kisses, and rushes to greet me when I come home. But are dogs capable of loving us back in the same way that we love them?

For thousands of years, "love" wasn't a concept that people thought of in connection with dogs. The initial relationships between early humans and wild canines most likely developed around a mutual need for food and an ability to help each other hunt. Dogs were more like work partners than cherished family members. But over the centuries, as the role of the dog evolved beyond a strictly business relationship, people began to become more emotionally attached to their canine companions.

Since the 1980s, dogs have rapidly moved from roles as backyard protectors to bedroom blanket stealers. We speak glowingly of how our dogs race to our front doors and greet us with smiling faces, swishing tails, and wiggling hips. We brag that our dogs comfort us when we feel blue and stay by our bedside when we are ill.

Are these acts of loyalty and devotion, or simply servitude and respect? Do our dogs rush to greet us because they are truly delighted by our return or because they need to go outside or want food? Do they remain by our side when we're sick because they truly care, or are they regarding us as members of their pack and acting out of a protective instinct?

In short, do dogs actually feel love and can they express this powerful emotion? While humans have conquered polio, landed astronauts on the moon, and created voice-activated computers, we have yet to come up with a scientific test to support or dispute the notion that dogs truly love us. I posed this question to Dr. Marty Becker, best known as America's Family Veterinarian, who is a major champion of the human-animal bond.

"Dogs truly love unconditionally," Dr. Becker says. "I think a dog's love is greater than human love. Dogs don't judge anyone. It you're bald or over-weight, it doesn't matter to a dog. Their sense of loyalty is tremendous."

Here are some ways dogs show their affection.

- Your dog makes sweet eye contact. His eyes are relaxed, not cold and staring.

- He responds excitedly to the sound of your voice and may drop his favorite chew toy the second you call his name or bring it to share with you as you enter the front door.

- He likes your scent. Scientists have shown that the scent of a favorite person triggers the reward center in a dog's brain known as the caudate nucleus.

- He wags his tail or does a full-body wiggle. Tail movement can signal various canine moods, but a happy back-and-forth wag with a loose, full-body wiggle is clearly communicating that you rock your dog's world.

- He does his best to lean and lie on you. Dogs can pick any place in the house to catnap or chill, but most of the time, they choose to cuddle with us. There's nothing better than sharing the sofa with your dog.

- He smiles at you. His mouth is open and relaxed as he focuses on his favorite two-legger—you.

While absolute scientific proof may be years away, I'm on Team Becker. Dogs do love us, and they show us their love in many ways. 🐾

Sniff It Out!

A dog's heart beats between 70 and 120 times a minute, compared with a human heart, which beats 70 to 80 times a minute.

THE DOG WILL SEE YOU NOW

The last few years have been difficult for our family. We've endured wicked storms, job changes, moving to a new house, and then the COVID-19 pandemic. Throughout these challenging times, we managed to smile and laugh thanks to Jackson, our boxer/Rottweiler mix. He is our constant source of positivity.

When I am dealing with a problem, he sits very attentively and will even gently touch my arm with his paw. He senses when I need to take a break for a dose of sunshine and will guide me to the door with a big grin. Sometimes, I feel like Jackson is more like my counselor than my dog.

Many dogs, like Jackson, are furry therapists who possess the ability to tap into our moods. Even Sigmund Freud, whose chow, Jo-Fi, was often present in sessions, recognized the therapeutic value that dogs offer to people. Study after study has shown that dogs can play a vital role in comforting and encouraging those who are suffering.

Our dogs often are able to shoo away the blues and turn sadness into gladness. They seem to recognize and care about our moods. They calm us down. They listen without interruption or judgment,

just like a psychologist. They can also succeed as four-legged cheerleaders and restore our self-confidence.

Dogs make great therapists because they provide unconditional empathy, positive regard, and genuineness. They are great listeners who don't judge. They allow us to talk out a problem and to let off some steam, which reduces our distress and lowers our blood pressure. This unqualified acceptance allows dogs to touch all types of people, from those experiencing mental or physical illnesses to those who simply live alone or who need motivation to prepare healthy meals for themselves.

Some dogs, like Kona, my terrier mix, complete training to be certified therapy dogs, a.k.a. canine goodwill ambassadors, who offer happiness to any and all, especially those in hospitals and in nursing homes. She is the most intuitive dog I've ever known, always able to correctly zero in on a person's emotional state and offer comfort.

Throughout history, dogs have served as confidants and emotional support systems for many people, including the famous and infamous. When Mary Queen of Scots was imprisoned in Fotheringhay Castle in England, she was denied human contact except for a priest and a servant woman, but she was permitted to keep her terrier, Geddon. As she approached the gallows to be beheaded, Mary hid her dog under her long skirt so he could be with her to the very end.

During World War II, General Dwight D. Eisenhower took Caacie, his Scottish terrier, with him during his North Africa tour. In letters to his wife, Mamie, Eisenhower remarked that Caacie was the only companion he could really talk to and the only one who would not turn the conversation back to the topic of war.

For everyday problems, nothing beats a canine pal. I know that when I return home feeling drained or depressed, my mood quickly lifts when Kona greets me with a full-body wiggle clutching her favorite toy in her mouth. It is hard not to break into a smile. 🐾

Paw Prints

Petting dogs is good for the soul! Among other services, trained therapy dogs bring joy to nursing home residents, encourage survivors of trauma to heal, provide solace to soldiers and emergency workers, and help struggling students learn to read and cope with stress.

SOLUTION FOR SERIOUS SHYNESS

We rescued an extremely shy young greyhound named Cyrus from a farm where he was kept in a barn for nearly the first year of his life. He and a bunch of other greyhounds were isolated from the world and left to starve by an uncaring breeder.

Cyrus acts anxious and submissive, and often cowers or slinks away when we try to pet him. He is afraid of everyday sights and sounds like vacuum cleaners and televisions. What can we do to boost his confidence and conquer his shyness?

Cyrus has a lot to process after his many months inside a very small world. He is still transitioning from those bad puppy days and has yet to realize that your home is both loving and permanent. It is important that you exercise lots of gentleness and patience with him. When I rescued Emma, a tiny dog found wandering our neighborhood with no identification, my veterinarian estimated that she was about 1 year old and showed signs of being abused.

For the first few months, Emma would pace nervously in the house, following me like a shadow. If I tried to pick her up, she would race to jump on the couch, where she felt safer, but would still shiver as I calmly petted her. If I spoke in a loud voice—perhaps overexcited by a great golf shot on television—she would go belly up and cower. It took about six months of gentle obedience training and consistent daily routines for Emma's true personality to begin to flourish. Happily, she is now a confident, affectionate buddy always happy to leash up for a walk and always ready to meet new people.

The same transformation can happen with Cyrus. Time is your ally as you and your family strive to earn his trust. It is common for submissive dogs to cower, avoid direct eye contact, and try to make themselves look smaller to avoid conflict. In extreme situations, they will tuck their tail between their legs and expose their bellies. In dog language, these actions convey that they are at the bottom of the family hierarchy and have no desire to challenge your place at the top.

Cyrus will gain confidence if you teach him the household rules with plenty of TLC and support. Start by not forcing him into any scary situations. Try to move slowly around him and let

24

him know that he can trust you to act consistently. Establish a routine for him and stick to it. Provide him with a crate or create a safe place for him in a corner where he can retreat with his back to a wall. Let him make the first moves for now.

If he musters the courage to come to you when you are sitting still, don't leap to reach out and touch him. Slowly extend your hand for him to sniff before accepting a gentle pet from you. Avoid patting the top of his head, as your

hand over him might feel like a threat. Your tone of voice is vital. Always use soft, upbeat, or warm tones. Never yell or speak harshly because you will only instill more fear.

Mealtime offers a special opportunity to shoo away Cyrus's shyness and bolster the bond between you. Hand-feed him his meals and treats. You may need to start one piece at a time. If he's too scared to take food from you at first, toss the treats a little bit away until

25

he gains confidence. If he backpedals, remain still until he returns to you.

Regular exercise will not only help Cyrus relax but also further develop your relationship. At first, stick to short walks around your immediate neighborhood. These outings will allow Cyrus to build up a database of familiar sights, sounds, and smells. If a car backfiring or other noise causes him to try to bolt, move him along quickly to distract him and give him the chance to settle down. Speak in a happy, confident tone while continuing your walk.

Inside your home or fenced backyard, engage Cyrus in some confidence-building activities like teaching him a trick with food rewards and plenty of praise. Don't make a big deal about appliances like the vacuum or dishwasher that may frighten him. If you treat them matter-of-factly, he will learn that they pose no threat. With consistently kind and gentle treatment, most shy dogs warm up and trust their immediate family members within a matter of weeks. You should begin to see Cyrus's true personality emerge pretty soon.

Once this occurs, I recommend you enroll him in a basic dog obedience class so he can have the chance to be around other dogs in a controlled setting. At this stage, you can also work on conquering Cyrus's shyness around newcomers to the house and strangers he meets when

he is out and about with you. Encourage your friends who visit not to make direct eye contact with Cyrus and to sit quietly.

As his confidence and curiosity take hold, have your friends offer him treats so he will form a positive association with visitors. Take things slowly and let Cyrus show you when he is ready to move on to the next stage of becoming a confident, happy dog. 🐾

Breed Byte

A greyhound with a white spot on her forehead will bring you good fortune, according to an old superstition. You may have better luck buying a lottery ticket if you want megadollars, but your dog is, of course, priceless.

PREPARING FOR PUPPY PANDEMONIUM

My husband and I are adopting a 12-week-old puppy. We want to make sure that our home is safe for him and from him! We have nice antiques and expensive rugs that we don't want chewed up or knocked over. Plus, we worry that the puppy could swallow something that could hurt him. How can we best prepare our home for our new family member?

You are wise to puppy-proof your house *before* your new family member comes home. Puppies are energetic and curious. In their first few months of life, one of the main ways they investigate is by taste-testing their surroundings. They demonstrate a real knack for getting into trouble and can quickly destroy household items and swallow things they shouldn't before you know it.

Start preparing your home for your bundle of joy by getting down on his level—literally. Sit down on the floor of each room where your puppy will be permitted to roam and look around for potential hazards that might be within his reach. These include electrical and telephone cords, houseplants on or near the floor, window shade and curtain drawstrings, throw rugs, trash cans or storage containers, and anything else on or near the floor that is small enough to fit into a puppy's mouth or light enough to be knocked over.

Think about materials such as wicker and cardboard that might not seem tempting to you but may attract a teething pup. Loose belongings such as shoes, toys, books, and magazines will be fair game at first, so form the habit of picking up clutter from the floors. (Having a puppy around can be a good incentive for messy children to put away their belongings!)

If you plan to give your puppy access to your kitchen or a bathroom, make sure cabinet doors near the floor are securely fastened. As a further precaution, consider storing all cleaning products and other toxic items in a higher location for now. A hanging shower curtain won't survive a puppy attack. Wrap it up high so it cannot be yanked down by your mischievous pup if he spends time alone in the bathroom.

Puppies can find trouble just about anywhere, so to start with, limit your pup's access to just two or three rooms of the house. The fewer rooms your puppy is allowed to visit, the less puppy-proofing you'll have to do. Once he grows out of the chewing stage and is reliably housebroken, you can gradually give him the run of the house. He has earned it!

By the way, many dogs happily learn to relax in a single room (kitchen, basement, or family room, for example) when the family is away, even though they are used to roaming around the rest of the time. You'll have a deeper and more satisfying relationship, however, with a dog who knows how to behave no matter where he is in the house, so don't rely on restricting his access as a permanent solution.

After checking the inside of your home for potential problems, step outdoors and review your backyard with your puppy in mind. Again, get down on his level by crouching down and checking out the view. Look for objects that your puppy can chew on and swallow, such as garden tools, children's toys, and other small objects. Pay close attention to your fencing to make certain there are no broken areas or gaps where your puppy could escape.

Puppies love to gnaw, and garden plants can be a tempting treat to a youngster exploring his world with his mouth. Take a look at the plant species in your yard and find out if any of them are poisonous to dogs. Any plant that is potentially toxic should be removed or blocked off with secure fencing, such as chicken wire. I recommend the ASPCA Animal Poison Control Center's website for a list of dog-friendly and dog-dangerous plants. This site is staffed 24-7 by board-certified veterinary toxicologists who can field any questions you have—and who often team up with family veterinarians to help dogs with poisoning issues.

Remember, too, that a rambunctious puppy can dig up a garden before you know what he's up to. If you have areas of soft dirt or sand in your yard, cover them by spreading out some chicken wire weighed down with large rocks to discourage the pup from digging.

Digging is a difficult habit to break, so it's best to prevent it from starting in the first place. Otherwise, your beautiful garden could end up looking like the surface of the moon.

For your puppy's safety, dispose of any pesticides or chemical fertilizers you might be using in your garden and switch to safer, more natural methods of pest control and plant feeding. Be particularly aware of poisonous bait designed to kill snails and slugs, as this can be very appealing to dogs and very deadly.

If your puppy will be allowed to keep you company while you are in your garage, pay special attention to puppy-proofing this area. Garages are notorious for housing hazardous chemicals that are deadly to pets. Antifreeze is a particular concern; look for a nontoxic brand. Tools, rags, car parts—anything that people normally keep in a garage—can become a danger if a puppy is around. Put these items well out of your puppy's reach.

In addition to puppy-proofing your property, you will need to provide your young pup with plenty of supervision, for safety's sake as well as for socialization. Tap the times you're with your pup to work in some fun training and games that will shape his manners and give him an appropriate outlet for his high energy. 🐾

An Ounce of Prevention

It takes time and effort, but puppy-proofing your house in the first place is much easier than rushing your puppy to the veterinarian for emergency surgery (not to mention the emotional and financial cost of such a trip). Veterinarians have removed a remarkable variety of objects from the stomachs and intestines of dogs of all ages, including pincushions (complete with pins), rubber balls, rocks, socks and underwear, ribbons, and plenty of splintered bones.

In most cases, a dog who dines without discretion and winds up on the operating table makes a full recovery, but any indigestible item can cause a potentially fatal intestinal blockage. Be alert to vomiting, distended abdomen, change in feces, drooling, or retching, and don't hesitate to take your dog to see your veterinarian if you suspect he's eaten something he shouldn't have.

LOOKING HANGDOG

My 10-year-old bichon frise sometimes goes to the bathroom in the house when no one is home. As soon as I walk in the front door, I know what Rascal has done without seeing the accident. She acts incredibly guilty, with downcast eyes and tail between her legs. If she feels so bad when she misbehaves, why does she continue to do this?

Also, I think she sometimes urinates on the floor to get even with me for being gone for too long. The longer I'm away from home, the more likely she is to have an accident. Is she trying to tell me something?

Many owners consider their pets to be members of the family, as well they should. But sometimes we take this idea too far by attaching human emotions and motives to our dog's behavior. Unlike humans, dogs don't feel guilty when they have done something we think is wrong. They do, however, react to our body language and tone of voice, and they quickly learn to read, and respond to, our emotions.

In Rascal's case, she has figured out that if she has an accident in the house, you will be angry when you get home, but she can't grasp a complicated thought like, "I had an accident and when Mom comes home in five hours and sees it, she'll get mad at me because now she has to clean it up, so I'd better hold it." Even though she's made that connection, she doesn't know *why* you're angry. Dogs have no concept of cause and effect, so unfortunately, she

doesn't realize that if she didn't go to the bathroom in the house, you would not be mad.

But if Rascal doesn't know she did something wrong, why does she look so guilty? Dogs often behave submissively when their owners are angry, in the hopes of ending the conflict. In wolf packs, subordinate members behave submissively in front of more dominant wolves to avoid fights. Rascal tucks her tail and hangs her head when she senses or anticipates your anger to illustrate her submissiveness to you, her pack leader. Signs of submissive behavior include a cringing posture, lowered ears, downcast eyes, and a tucked tail. A canine pack leader would most likely accept this behavioral apology and move on. Unhappily, people tend to become even angrier when confronted by such signs of "guilt," which makes the poor dog cringe even more.

As for the possibility of Rascal going to the bathroom in the house to get even with you for leaving her alone too long, dogs do not have the capacity to think in these terms. Revenge remains an exclusive human endeavor, and something only a complex brain can calculate. Dogs don't have the mental ability or the emotional complexity to grasp the concept of getting even.

Rascal's accidents are most likely the result of her inability to hold her urine for long periods of time. Certain breeds, with the bichon frise topping the list, are considered challenging to potty train. Older dogs often have trouble with incontinence and sometimes need medication to remedy the problem. She may be suffering from a urinary tract infection or another medical condition that makes it hard for her to hold a full bladder for an extended period of time.

Take Rascal to your veterinarian for a complete physical evaluation. In the meantime, try not to leave her alone for too long to help her avoid accidents. This might mean asking a neighbor or professional pet sitter to come over and let her out in the yard to relieve herself on days you know you'll be gone for a long period of time. 🐾

Breed Byte

The white, powder-puff bichon frise takes its name from a French term that means "curly lapdog."

CAN YOU DIG IT?

My 5-year-old German shepherd/Lab mix has destroyed my garden with her digging. My yard looks like a minefield. I don't know what to do to stop her. As soon as we fill up the holes, Greta digs them up again. Why is she so obsessed with digging, and how can we make her stop?

I'm sure you've noticed how much Greta seems to enjoy herself when she digs. Many dogs love to dig in soft dirt or sand. In the wild, wolves and other canids dig to create dens for their pups or to hide food. The instinct to dig remains strong in many domestic dogs who bury their bones or toys and scratch out cool places to rest during the summertime heat. Some dogs dig to burn off energy and relieve boredom. Unfortunately, digging, while not harmful to the dog, is destructive behavior that leaves owners frustrated and dogs in big trouble.

Before you can fix Greta's digging problem, you need to understand her motivation for digging. Does she spend a lot of time alone in your backyard? Do you take the time to play with her? Is she exercised regularly? Both German shepherds and Labrador retrievers are high-energy breeds who need plenty of activity and mental stimulation to wear them out. If you don't provide something for a dog like Greta to do, she will make her own fun, most likely in a way you don't appreciate. This is probably why she has taken up digging.

Digging can be a difficult habit to break, because dogs like to do it. The key to fixing this problem is to give Greta less destructive ways to burn off her energy while also discouraging her from tearing up the yard. It's time to make a deal with your gotta-dig dog.

Create a digging site in your yard that is far more beckoning to Greta than your flower bed or grassy lawn. Dedicate a certain corner of your yard as Greta's digging place, and encourage her to dig there only. You can fill an inexpensive plastic kiddy pool with soft dirt or sand and hide a few dog treats for Greta to sniff out and enjoy. Think of it as a canine treasure hunt. Be sure to heap on the praise each time she digs in this designated place.

At the same time, make the rest of the yard less welcoming. Drop some of Greta's poop in the holes she dug in your lawn and then cover them with dirt. Sprinkle the area with red pepper flakes or spray it with citronella to make the area even less appealing. Greta's nose will tell her that is not a nice spot to dig. Protect your garden areas by fencing them off with chicken wire to block her access.

If you have time—and Greta is game—consider getting involved in a fun, competitive canine activity like agility or fly ball. Greta would no doubt love one of these high-energy sports. (See page 142 for more on canine sports.) 🐾

NIPPING THE HERDING INSTINCT

We have a 2-year-old Shetland sheepdog named Casey. She is a wonderful dog except for one thing: She chases our three young children. When the kids run and play in the backyard, Casey goes after them and nips at their heels. This really upsets the kids and they start to cry. Casey has torn their clothing, and I'm afraid she is going to accidentally hurt one of them. Why does she do this and how can we stop her?

Shetland sheepdogs belong to the class of herding breeds, which range in size from the shaggy Old English sheepdog to the stubby-legged corgi. My old corgi, Jazz, took great delight in rounding up my cats whenever one dared to slip through the doggy door into the backyard. He would herd the frustrated feline back to the door and sound the alert for me to check out his successful mission.

In your situation, Casey is simply fulfilling the legacy of her breed.

Shelties were bred to herd livestock in their native Shetland Islands, off the coast of Scotland. They helped farmers move sheep from one pasture to another and along country roads to market. To get the sheep to comply, the dogs chased and nipped at their heels. Unfortunately, without sheep to attend to, Casey has chosen to herd your children. The rapid, erratic movements of children playing often trigger a herding dog's instincts.

33

This herding tendency is difficult, if not impossible, to suppress. Hundreds of years of breeding went into creating Casey's behavior, so it's not something she can just turn off. One solution is to use another form of play to divert her attention. When the kids start playing, engage Casey in a game of fetch. Many herding breed dogs will gladly give up trying to herd unruly children in favor of chasing a tennis ball or nosing a soccer ball or an empty plastic jug around the yard.

Of course, this only works if you are around to supervise. If you don't have time to play with her while the kids are running around the yard, your best approach is to remove the temptation and keep Casey in the house while the children are playing.

It's very likely, however, that Casey won't appreciate being shut out of the fun and will bark and whine at the door. Don't let her develop another bad habit! Practice some obedience work with her to shift her attention from the children. If she refuses to be diverted, move her into a room where she can't see or hear the kids playing. If Casey is crate-trained, this would be a good time to make use of the crate. Put her in the crate with a treat or toy and let her stay there until the kids have gone on to a more sedate activity.

But do make sure that she has plenty of other opportunities to run and play—she is a young dog with lots of energy to burn. I recommend you spend 5 to 10 minutes each day encouraging Casey to practice herding acceptable objects, such as a soccer ball or football, around the yard instead.

However you choose to deal with this situation, it's imperative that you do something to stop Casey's behavior. Although your dog may not intend to hurt your children, her nipping and chasing may well result in injury to one of your children or to one of their friends. 🐾

HAVE NOSE, MUST TRAVEL

Whenever I take my beagle, Wesley, on a hike, his ears seem to stop working. We spent a long time in obedience class learning all the commands, and at home and in the park, he listens well. But when I take him on our weekend hikes to a local wilderness area and remove his leash, it's as though I don't exist. He puts his nose to the ground and takes off.

I can yell, *Wesley, come!* until I lose my voice, but it does no good. I end up having to run after him and physically grab him to get his attention. I worry that he'll become so engrossed in sniffing that he will wander off and get hit by a car or get lost. Why does he act like this?

Beagles, like all hound breeds, were bred specifically to track prey by following scent. The breed has been used for hundreds of years to hunt fox, rabbits, squirrels, and other small game. Hunters on horseback follow packs of these dogs, depending on them to locate the prey and corner it until the hunters can make the kill.

The olfactory power of Wesley's nose is about 10,000 times stronger than yours. That profound ability to detect the faintest scent, combined with hundreds of years of breeding to track prey, has created a dog that becomes completely focused on finding and hunting down game, no matter how many times you shout his name. This makes it tricky to control Wesley off leash in a wilderness setting where the scent of rabbits, squirrels, and other animals prevails over your voice. So far, you've been lucky that you've been able to catch him. Many beagles run off after a scent and get themselves good and lost, sometimes permanently.

You have a good foundation of obedience training at home, but now you need to work on training him to come when called while in that distracting environment. Whatever you do, don't let him disregard your call. If you repeat *Come* over and over again while he ignores you, you are only teaching him that he doesn't have to listen.

Because you must be able to reinforce the cue if Wesley isn't listening, begin working with him on a leash when you take him on hikes. Use a 25-foot clothesline, rather than a standard 6-foot leash. The longer line allows you to gradually give Wesley more distance between you as you work on teaching him to come when called from farther away, despite the distractions. Make sure that you select a wide-open area without trees or other objects that can tangle the leash.

Bring treats with you on your training sessions, and start by giving Wesley six feet of clothesline. Wait until he starts sniffing around, and then give him the *Come* command. If he responds and comes to you, praise him heartily and give him a treat, and let him go off again. If he doesn't respond, "reel" him in on the line, but don't give him a treat. (Don't yell at him either!) When he is paying attention to you and coming reliably on six feet of line, give him a couple more feet of clothesline so he's farther away from you, and repeat the exercise.

If he ignores you, pull him toward you to make him come, but do not reward him when he gets to you. Go back to a shorter amount of line and start over.

With practice, you should have Wesley responding when you call him from the end of the 25-foot rope, each and every time. Once this is accomplished, you can try removing the leash to see if he will still come to you. Ultimately, you should gain more control over Wesley as he learns that he cannot continue whatever he is doing when you say *Come*.

Because beagles have such strong scenting and tracking instincts, however, Wesley may never be completely reliable off leash in a wilderness area. If this turns out to be the case, keep him leashed when you are hiking, for his own protection. (Make sure his collar has up-to-date tags. You might look into microchipping him as well.) Despite the stories of dogs finding their way home, most lost dogs, even ones with above-average scenting abilities, stay lost. 🐾

Paw Prints

At the end of the Beatles song "A Day in the Life," Paul McCartney recorded an ultrasonic whistle, audible only to dogs, as a message for his Shetland sheepdog.

Let's See Some ID

Think of a microchip as your dog's driver's license. No dog should be without one. Although you can provide your dog's name and your contact info on tags and even embroidered on their collars, these methods are not as effective as microchipping. All it takes is an open door for a dog to suddenly find himself lost. If your dog loses his tags and collar, the chances of being reunited with you become slim. A microchip is permanent.

I encourage all dog owners to book appointments with their veterinarians to microchip their dogs. The procedure is quick and requires no anesthesia. A chip less than the size of a grain of rice is inserted under the skin (usually between the shoulder blades) with a special needle.

More and more veterinary clinics and animal shelters have special wands that they can wave over found dogs to detect these microchips, which have identification numbers that are registered with a national database. With the ID number, your dog's contact information is available to the clinic or shelter.

Please be sure to register with the company who makes the specific microchip used in your dog. If you move or change your phone number, remember to update your contact information.

SEEKING THE RIGHT CANINE

I'm looking for a friendly, fun-loving dog to adopt, but I live in a one-bedroom apartment in a major city. I really don't think it is an ideal place for a high-energy, big dog like a Labrador retriever or a German shepherd. But I really don't want an itty-bitty dog, either. Any recommendations? I am open to adopting at a breed rescue group or an animal shelter, but I do want a dog that is a particular breed.

Selecting the right canine for you and your lifestyle should be done with purpose. After all, you are most likely to have this dog longer than the car you now drive and maybe even your current job. Whether you decide to get a purebred dog from a reputable breeder or a breed rescue group or adopt a dog from an animal shelter, take this quiz to help find the right dog for you.

○ Is your lifestyle more "go, go, go" or "kick back and relax"? Match your energy level with each canine contender. Surprisingly, swift dogs like greyhounds spend more time snoozing on the sofa

than small terrier mixes who have plenty of energy for running and playing.

- Do you like the sun or snow? If you enjoy warm weather and want your dog to join you, be careful if you select one with a short, pushed-in face (known as *brachycephalic*) because these dogs can overheat quickly. You will need to keep outdoor walks and training sessions short when the temperature climbs. If you dig the snow, consider a dog with a double coat or a thick coat to help insulate him from dropping temperatures when you are both outside.

- Will your dog sleep on your bed? Be aware that some dogs with short snouts have reputations as snorers. And some dogs, such as mastiffs and boxers, are major droolers, so your pillow may be soggy when you wake up. Decide early on if your dog will join you on your bed or if you will treat him to a comfy bed of his own in your bedroom.

- How are your grooming skills? If you do not wish to spend a lot of time keeping your dog's coat looking its best, consider a short-haired breed instead of one that sheds a lot or one that requires daily brushing and professional grooming appointments. Remember, the skin is your dog's biggest organ. Keeping the skin and coat healthy goes a long way in keeping the total dog healthy.

- How big is your wallet? There is no such thing as a free dog, even if you rescue a stray. All dogs need quality chow, comfy bedding, toys, leashes, and of course regular veterinary care. Make sure you factor canine costs into your family budget before deciding to add a dog to your home.

As for me, my canine pack includes a trio of mutts: Kona, a Jack Russell terrier/whippet combo; Emma, a terrier blend; and Bujeau, a Bernese mountain dog/Catahoula leopard dog mix. My favorite purebred is the Pembroke Welsh corgi, a short-legged, long-backed canine of the herding group and a royal favorite of Queen Elizabeth. My late, great Jazz was a corgi, and I affectionately describe corgis as a cross between Robin Williams and the Three Stooges due to their brilliant comedic personalities.

Wishing you the very best in finding the right four-legged pal! 🐾

Breed Byte

Ancient folklore says that the Pembroke Welsh corgi (*corgi* means "dwarf" in Welsh) was a gift from the woodland fairies and that the breed still carries the marks of fairy harnesses on its coat.

POOF! DISAPPEARING DOG ACT

Our 6-year-old Siberian husky, Tundra, is always escaping from our yard. He used to dig under the fence, so we reinforced it all around the bottom, but then he found a way to open the gate. We put a lock on the gate, and now he jumps over the fence. No matter what we do to stop him, he finds a way to escape.

We have finally started locking him in the garage when we aren't home because we got tired of going to the animal shelter to pick him up. Why does he run away? Should we take this as a sign that he doesn't like living here?

Tundra sounds like a tenacious escape artist who is determined to spend his time checking out the neighborhood. It's doubtful that this is because he doesn't like living with you. It's more likely that when he's alone, he feels compelled to provide his own amusement. The fact that Tundra is a Siberian husky also contributes to his tendency to roam. Huskies were bred to travel vast distances pulling sleds and to think for themselves while they worked. When Tundra decides to leave your yard, he is responding to his inbred urge to travel and be independent.

I share your love for huskies. When I first adopted my wonderful husky/golden retriever mix, Chipper, her husky heritage frequently encouraged her to disappear from my yard, but the golden retriever in her seemed to coax her back to my front porch. I used to say, "The husky in her wants to roam, but the golden in her wants to stay home."

You can take several steps to curb Tundra's roaming, in addition to the excellent measures you have already employed. First, make sure Tundra is neutered. Male dogs are notorious for doing everything possible to escape their homes in order to search for females in heat. If Tundra is still intact, this could be the biggest source of your problem. Have him neutered right away and keep him confined until his raging hormones subside.

It sounds like Tundra performs his escape routines when you aren't home and he's alone in the backyard. He is probably bored or lonely or both. Before you leave him for long periods of time, give him some vigorous exercise to tire him out. A rousing game of fetch or a long jog (if you are so inclined) can do wonders to burn off some of his excess energy and make him less likely to run away. Physical exercise and mentally stimulating games will also improve Tundra's confidence level.

Loneliness can also motivate a dog to escape his yard in the hopes of finding companionship. Huskies, more than many breeds, are pack animals, bred to work in a group and to be around other dogs. Try hiring a professional pet sitter or a responsible, dog-friendly neighborhood teen to come over in the afternoon to take Tundra for a walk or play fetch

with him in the yard. Breaking up the isolation of his day will help reduce his desire to leave your yard in search of companionship. If you have the room and the financial ability, a compatible second dog might be the perfect solution.

Tundra's attitude will probably benefit from some training as well. Enroll him in an obedience class so both you and he can learn the basics. Obedience training will reinforce the bond between you and Tundra and help him see you as his pack leader. If Tundra feels more connected to you emotionally, he'll be less likely to want to leave your home.

In addition, you might want to secure your yard even further to help stave off any more of Tundra's escape attempts. Since he has taken to jumping over the fence, consider adding wire at the top that is slanted inward at a 90-degree angle to the fence. Tundra will find it very difficult, if not impossible, to jump over the fence with this extension blocking his exit. 🐾

Paw Prints

Laika, a Siberian husky mix, was the first dog in space. The Soviets launched her aboard Sputnik II in 1957. *Laika* is Russian for "bark."

STOP, SHOE THIEF!

My 3-year-old Lab mix, Schotzi, goes into my closet when I'm not home and takes my shoes out to chew on them. I try to keep the closet door closed, but if I inadvertently leave it open even just a few inches, she pushes it open with her nose and drags out a shoe and destroys it. Why is she so obsessed with shoes, and how can I stop this bad (and expensive) habit?

I'm guessing the shoes in your closet that Schotzi prefers are made of leather. Many dogs find the smell and texture of leather intoxicating. They love the way it feels and tastes when they chew on it. Some people make the mistake of giving old shoes to puppies to chew on when they are little, expecting the pup to know the difference between an old shoe that's okay to chew and a newer shoe that is off-limits.

If Schotzi was given old shoes to gnaw on when she was little, she learned at a young age that shoes are made for chewing. Now, when she wants to gnaw on something, she simply helps herself from your wardrobe.

Even if you didn't give Schotzi shoes when she was a puppy, she is choosing something that smells like you and that reassures her in your absence. Many dogs deal with loneliness or separation anxiety by seeking out their owner's belongings (to dogs, a stinky shoe is a particularly comforting reminder of their owners).

Your first task is to make sure you don't tempt her by leaving your closet door ajar. You might try putting self-closing hinges on the closet door or even closing your bedroom door as well. You could store your shoes on shelves above her reach or in a hanging container with pockets.

Next, give her something else to chew. Consider healthy, long-lasting items, such as carrots, canine dental chews, or bully sticks. Avoid rawhides, as small pieces can break off and cause choking. Chewing on them can also chip teeth.

Just before you leave the house, give Schotzi one of these safe chews or a Kong toy stuffed with small treats. Praise her heartily when she starts working on it. If she isn't interested at first, a dab of peanut butter or a smear of cheese on the chew will probably increase its attractiveness.

In the event that Schotzi does sink her teeth into one of your shoes and you catch her in the act, take it away from her (Have you taught her the *Leave it!* command? See Ignoring Temptation, page 129.) and trade it for another item to chew. In time she will get the

message that shoes are a no and safe chews are a yes.

You may need to try different chews and toys to shift Schotzi's attention from your shoes. To make the transition, try bringing her with you to a pet supply store. Walk her through the aisles and see which chew toys interest her the most. By letting her pick out her own toy, you are making her an active participant in her retraining. 🐾

Paw Prints

The first doggy day care opened in New York City in 1987, created by a frustrated college student looking for a suitable fun place for his puppy while he attended classes. Now the number of doggy day care centers in the United States tops 500.

UNDERCOVER AGENT

My dachshund, Bogart, makes us laugh with his bedtime ritual. It doesn't matter if the weather is warm or cold, he insists on burying his entire body under the covers and sleeping at our feet. To make it a challenge, we've tried making the bed so that the sheets and bedspread are tucked in tightly, but he still manages to wiggle his way under the sheets. Sometimes I worry that he won't get enough oxygen being so deep under the covers. Why does he do this and can it be harmful?

Bogart belongs to a great breed that was born to dig. Although they are affectionately known as "wiener dogs" because of their long backs and short legs, *dachshund* actually means "badger dog" in German. These bold, funny, curious, and determined dogs were bred to dig for burrowing mammals and to boldly take on badgers and other large varmints, climbing out of the hole triumphantly clutching their prey in their mouths. Designed so that their teeth—not their toes—are the first body parts that come in contact with prey deep in a hole, dachshunds are fierce fighters.

As for the bedtime ritual, wiggling into tight places (like under the covers) comes naturally to Bogart and feels cozy. As long as he doesn't disturb your sleep or nip your toes, let him continue this nighttime ritual. Don't worry—he can breathe under the sheets and will emerge if he becomes uncomfortable. 🐾

TOSSING AND TWITCHING ALL NIGHT

My family gets the biggest kick out of watching our 6-year-old Lab, Barnaby, sleep. Not only does he snore—loudly—but also his outstretched paws move and he twitches all over. Sometimes he yelps or whimpers, but his eyes stay closed. Watching and listening to him when he is sleeping makes us wonder if dogs dream and, if so, what do they dream about?

Compared with us, dogs are regular Rip Van Winkles. They sleep at least twelve hours a day and rarely suffer from insomnia. At night, they seem to nod off before you even have time to set your snooze alarm. Not all dogs snore like Barnaby, but it is fairly common for dogs to twitch their paws and make noises when they are asleep. Some dogs move their legs as if they were in full stride, perhaps chasing a rabbit.

Look closely at Barnaby and you might also notice the twitching of his eyelids and whiskers, indicating that he has fallen into the deep sleep stage. But dogs don't stay in that deep slumber for long. Most of the time, they sleep lightly and are aware of their surroundings.

Sleep experts report that dogs do indeed dream. The big mystery is their topics of choice when they drift off into dreamland. We can only guess that they dream about trips to the dog park, chowing down on their favorite treat, or finally catching a speedy, elusive squirrel.

Some scientists speculate that dogs may dream primarily of smells. That holds merit. After all, we dream visually because sight is our dominant sense. Dogs rely on their noses more than their eyes. They smell objects before they see, hear, touch, or taste them. It may be a long time before we figure out a way to identify our dogs' dreams, but it is a strong bet that since much of a dog's brain is associated with scents, it is a dream filled with lots of canine-welcoming smells.

STASHING AWAY FOR A RAINY DAY

My Brittany spaniel, Chelsea, has a weird food habit. When I feed her kibble, she picks up each piece from her bowl and places it on the kitchen floor or in other rooms of the house. After she has removed all the kibble from her bowl, she tracks down each piece throughout the house and eats it. Why does she do this?

Chelsea's odd eating habits are a throwback to her ancient roots as a hunter and scavenger. Chelsea's ancestors could not count on people to serve them two meals each day. Because food was not always available to wolves and other wild dogs whenever they needed it, they would stash parts of their kill in various places so they could return to it later when they were hungry and couldn't find prey. Some domestic dogs, particularly hunting breeds like spaniels, still retain this instinct. In fact, some dogs will actually hide each piece of kibble in corners or under furniture before they go back and eat it.

Even though Chelsea receives regular meals, this ancient instinct is telling her to stash the kibble in different places so she can return to it later to eat it. Of course, "later" may only be a few minutes after she has performed her food-relocation ritual. But in Chelsea's mind, her behavior helps ensure a constant source of food in the future. To human observers, this food-spreading behavior doesn't make sense unless you think about the instinct that is driving it. Just remember as you watch Chelsea spread her food around that she is heeding the call of the wild.

If you don't want kibble surprises all over your house, I recommend you use doggy gates during mealtime to limit Chelsea's spreading turf to the kitchen area. At the very least, keep bedroom and bathroom doors closed during feeding time. Stepping on hard kibble with bare feet is no delight! 🐾

Breed Byte

The earliest Irish setters were actually red and white. The solid red type first appeared in Ireland in the nineteenth century.

What Are You TALKING ABOUT?

It's easy to fall into the notion that people are superior to the rest of the animal kingdom because of our ability to talk. Some of us speak more than one language. Some of us know many multisyllabic words and can even pronounce most of them. Some of us, in fact, never seem to stop talking! That's all fine and good when it comes to speaking person-to-person.

As much as we may view ourselves as accomplished linguists, the truth is that our dogs are the truly stellar communicators, often without uttering a single bark or yip. In dog-to-dog discussions, there is rarely a communication miscue. Dogs are more consistent in their "talk" than we are. They don't tell lies, and they don't hide their feelings.

Dogs do their best to convey their canine cues to us, but sometimes we fail to interpret their signals accurately. There are "doggy lingo" or "bark-o" language apps to help us learn to speak dog. But we can improve our communication with our canine pals if we learn some of their "language." Along the way, we may commit a canine "faux paw" or two, but that's all right. After all, we're only human.

CANINE CONVERSATION

My dog is a very vocal miniature schnauzer. At times, it seems like we are actually carrying on a conversation. I never knew that dogs could make so many different sounds. She has several different barks, she whines, and she even makes singing sounds. How can I better understand what she is saying?

Miniature schnauzers are among the chattiest of breeds. Like many of their terrier cousins, they were bred to alert their owners to rodents in the home and while going to ground after small game. Beagles and other hound breeds bark to answer back to their two-legged hunting companions. Corgis, Australian shepherds, and other herding breeds yap to control the comings and goings of sheep, cattle, and other livestock.

Although dogs communicate primarily with nonverbal body language, they are capable of a wide range of sounds. There is always a purpose for their barks, even if the reason is sheer boredom. These sounds have consistent meanings, based on the pitch, pace, and overall tones.

Here are some common dog sounds.

High-pitched, long, repeated bark. "I'm worried or lonely and need assurance."

Rapid, high-pitched, repetitive barks. "Let's play! Chase me! At least throw my ball!"

Low, repetitive barks. "Stay away from my family! Keep off my property!"

A single bark or two. "Hey! I'm here! What are you doing?"

Growling with teeth exposed and tense body leaning forward. "I'm warning you—back off and leave me alone."

Growling with body crouched low. "You're making me nervous. If you come too close, I might snap at you."

Singsong howling. "Hey, calling all canines! Who's out there? What's going on?"

Squeaky, repetitive yaps or whines. "I'm hurt or scared or feeling stressed. I need attention!"

The Name Game

Stumped by what to call your new dog? You can go with the majority by choosing Molly or Max—two of the most popular canine monikers. If you want to be more original, here are some recommendations to make sure the name aptly fits.

- Stick with a two-syllable name ending in a vowel, like Buddy or Gracie.

- Select a name you enjoy saying out loud like Keeper or Eddie—not an embarrassing name like Poopsie or Dingaling.

- Consider names associated with something you enjoy. If you're a golfer, go with a positive name like Putter or Chipper, not a negative one like Divot or Bogey.

- Avoid names that sound like *no* such as Joe or Flo.

- Take some time and link the name to your dog's personality such as Happy, Frisky, or Speedy.

Whatever name you choose, make sure your dog associates hearing you speak his name with positive experiences. Say the name when you play, feed, and cuddle with your new dog so that he begins to recognize his canine identity. Resist using his name when you need to stop a behavior like digging or barking.

OKAY TO GROWL IN PLAY?

When I play fetch with a tennis ball with my 2-year-old golden retriever, she sometimes lets out a little *grrr* sound. She looks at me with a silly look on her face. She has an open-mouth grin, puts her butt high in the air, and stretches her front paws out in front. Even though she is growling, it seems like she's being playful. Or is she challenging me?

It is key to your safety that you read your dog's total body posture message. Far too often, people zero in on a wagging tail and think that is the human equivalent of a happy handshake. Wrong. Pay attention to your dog's facial expressions and look out for any signs of body tensing.

A growl is a vital communication tool for dogs. There are happy growls and warning "back off" growls. It is important to properly interpret the growl in the context of the situation. From the body postures you describe, your dog is delivering a happy growl because she is excited to be playing with you. She is showing you the "play bow" position (front legs splayed out, head lowered, rear end elevated). Her alert expression and soft vocalizations are friendly invites for you to continue trying to grab the ball from her and tossing it. She regards you as a valued playmate. Her "growls" are her way of declaring,

"I love playing fetch with you." Such happy growls are made by dogs playing tug with their favorite people or canine pals as well.

However, if she were emitting a deep, long, low *grrr* sound with her lips pulled back, that is not a friendly signal. This type of growl is a warning sound and, unheeded, may be followed by a bite. Some dogs also growl when they are afraid. Their ears are flattened and pinned back, and their tails are tucked.

The good news is that most dogs go through life without growling at anyone.

Use playtime to your advantage to instill clear communication with your dog and to hone her good manners. When your dog is in a playful mood, reinforce some basic behaviors, such as *Sit* and *Stay*. (See Training Tips, page 208.) Have your dog heed these cues before getting a reward, in this case, the tennis ball. Finally, you decide when the game is over, not your dog. This reinforces your position as leader. 🐾

STRICTLY DOG-TO-DOG

Whenever my husky mix, Jessie, meets a new dog, she goes through a whole ritual of posturing. Usually, the hair on her spine goes up. She marches up to the newcomer at our dog park in silence. She sniffs the dog's rear end and often places her head over the other dog's back. Sometimes she will make a few quick growling noises, but within a few seconds the two are playing chase and then sharing a water bowl.

I know my dog is not aggressive, but I find myself always having to explain to other dog owners that this is just how Jessie meets other dogs. Is this normal dog behavior?

Jessie behaves a lot like Chipper, my late, great husky mix, did in canine intros. When excited or threatened, the hair—or hackles—spike up along the back, especially in certain breeds, like huskies. The official term to describe this is piloerection—think of it as the canine equivalent of getting goose bumps.

Also at play is Jessie's personality. She is a confident, dominant female. There is a big difference between being dominant and being aggressive. Dominant dogs are outgoing and assertive. Aggressive dogs, however, stare intensely, pin their ears back, display stiff tails held high, and lean forward with tense bodies.

At any dog park, you'll find a wide gamut of dog personalities with various levels of social skills. And there is a wide spectrum of people, from those paying attention to their dogs and their body cues to those who are too consumed by looking at their phones to pay attention to their dogs and intervene before a fight erupts.

When dogs first meet, they often quickly size up each other without a single bark. They sniff each other, eye each other, and within seconds know each other's sex, age, health condition, and position on the canine hierarchy.

And just as you described, the dominant dog will hold her head over the back of the submissive one. There is a moment of stillness as the two dogs study one another. Both understand this posturing and generally accept their social rankings. Sometimes a brief scuffle will break out, usually over in seconds, but sometimes a serious fight can ensue.

This form of behavior is far different from when two canine chums greet one another. During friendly reunions, familiar dogs will sniff each other's faces and rear ends but may also jump up and touch front paws in midair or playfully mouth their pal's neck or tug on their cheek. Notice their mouths. Happy, relaxed dogs keep their mouths open. Tense, alert dogs keep their mouths tightly closed.

Even though you describe Jessie as not aggressive, pay close attention to new doggy introductions at the dog park and other places. If the other dog turns out to be aggressive, especially fearful aggressive, you need to be close enough to be able to break up a fight if necessary.

I applaud you for taking Jessie for social outings and for focusing on her during this playtime. It gives both of you an opportunity to live in the moment outside in the fresh air, and you are learning to read her body language, which makes for a stronger bond between you. 🐾

How to Safely Break Up a Dogfight

No one goes out on a dog walk looking for a fight. But while you are with your leashed dog, a loose dog may charge at you and attack your dog. Or your dog may react aggressively if a strange dog approaches, and suddenly you have a snarling, snapping mess at your feet. Breaking up a dogfight can be dangerous. Never attempt to separate the two dogs by reaching in and grabbing a collar—you are apt to be bitten.

Here are some tips.

- Carry thumb-sized treats that you can toss away from you and your dog. Try to lure the charging dog away from you and toward the treats.

- If you had your dog on a leash prior to the fight, keep it on—it's better for control.

- Stay calm. That's easier said than done, because a dogfight is pretty frightening and intense; realize, however, that yelling at the dogs will increase their anxiety. Speaking in a strong voice, say "No" or tell your dog to stop.

- Avoid hitting the dogs or getting your hands anywhere near their mouths. Hitting could make the situation worse and could cause the attack to be redirected toward you.

- Distract the dogs if you're unable to pull them away from each other. Use a noisemaking device such as an air horn to drive them apart, pour water on them, or throw a blanket or jacket on them to disorient them. Spray the aggressor with a hose if handy, aiming for the nostrils. This works well if you are working alone to pull two or more dogs apart.

- Enlist another person to help you separate the dogs by grabbing their hind legs and walking them backward like wheelbarrows; be careful not to hold the legs in such a way that the dog can just turn around and bite you. Once separated, secure the dogs away from each other before releasing them. Walk them away from each other as soon as you can; don't even let them make eye contact.

Once you are in a safe place, thoroughly inspect your dog from head to tail. Puncture wounds can be hard to find and can quickly become swollen and infected. Take your dog to your veterinarian for treatment if you find any injuries.

ARE DOGS WORD WORTHY?

When I talk to my dog, Charlie, he usually cocks his head, as if he is really listening and understanding what I'm telling him. Do dogs know words, or is he just listening to the tone of my voice?

Dogs read your voice tone, more than the actual words, to gauge if you're delivering praise or discipline. Try this test with Charlie. Stiffen your muscles, grab a cookbook and begin to call out names of different foods in a stern, low tone in front of him. Watch his response. I bet he will glance your way, crouch down, and move away from you, almost as if to say, "I can tell you're angry about something but I'm not sure why."

Now, repeat the exercise, but this time, relax your muscles, sit on the floor, and call out the food names in a cheery, musical tone. Watch what Charlie does. He will probably race over to you with a circular wag and a happy, open-mouth grin and try to give you kisses.

Although the same words spoken in a different tone elicit different reactions from your dog, many dogs do understand specific words and phrases. That's because we have been consistent when speaking these words. In addition to learning cues such as *Sit*, *Stay*, and *Come*, many dogs soon realize what you're talking about when you say *Treat*, *Walk*, or *Toy*, even if you spell out the words. (See Spelling Champ, page 58.)

You can train your four-legged vocabulary builder to perform some nifty tricks by using treats and praise to reinforce desired responses. For example, let's say you want to wow your pals when they visit by telling them that your dog is multilingual. I have trained my terrier mix, Kona, in the basics of *Sit*, *Stay*, *Down*, and *Come* in English, Spanish, and hand gestures.

She has learned that whether I say *Park it* in English or *Sientate* in Spanish or I raise my hand palm side up, I'm asking her to get into a sit. When I want her to stay, she comprehends that *Whoa* and *Quieto* and my open palm held up like a traffic cop all mean for her to stay and not move. Each time, Kona breaks through the language barrier and aces the cue. 🐾

Paw Prints

Chanda-Leah, a toy poodle, put her paw prints in history and made it into the *Guinness Book of World Records* by snaring the world record for being able to perform the most tricks—469 and counting.

Chaser and Stella: Word Wonder Dogs

A pair of smart canines named Chaser and Stella demonstrate that dogs can comprehend many more words than we realize and use them to engage in two-way communication with us. Animal behaviorists estimate that smart dogs can comprehend more than 165 words.

But the word record may belong to Chaser, a border collie dubbed the "smartest dog in the world" because she knew more than 1,000 words! Her pet parent, John Pilley, a retired college psychology professor, schooled Chaser with hours of fun play and positive reinforcement. Instead of cognition, Professor Pilley used "dognition" to hone and test Chaser's vocabulary talents.

In her 15 years of life, Chaser memorized the names of more than 1,000 toys and could retrieve the requested one more than 90 percent of the time. Professor Pilley, who passed away in 2018, wrote a book called *Chaser: Unlocking the Genius of the Dog Who Knows a Thousand Words*. He was one of my favorite guests on my podcast *Oh Behave!* on Pet Life Radio.

In the next generation of dogs with big vocabularies, Stella, a blue heeler/Catahoula mix, is billed as the world's first talking dog. Her pet parent,

Christina Hunger, is a speech-language pathologist. She introduced Stella to a special communication device she uses with her human clients. The tail-wagger with the big ears has learned to press specific buttons to voice her thoughts and requests (more treats, want outside), and she can create phrases up to five words long! Check out videos of her and other button-pushing canines on YouTube.

Chaser could reliably recognize more than 1,000 words.

SPELLING CHAMP

Our dog gets so excited when she hears the words *treat* or *walk* that we've started to spell them out. But now it seems like she understands when we say "t-r-e-a-t" or "w-a-l-k." She starts to jump around, wiggle, and squeal with delight. We are amazed that she responds. Is our dog a speller?

Many dog owners try to outwit their dogs by coming up with a secret code for highly prized objects, such as a treat, walk, or car ride. It is natural to switch to spelling to tone down the emotional outbursts of pure delight from a dog on constant alert for his favorite words. But think about how these words became such favorites in the first place. Dogs quickly learn to associate the word *treat* with the tasty biscuit or dog cookie that you hand over. They soon catch on that *walk* leads to you reaching for the leash and heading to the front door.

By spelling out these key words every time you provide a treat or take her for a trek to the park, your dog links these sounds with their meanings. She can't spell, but she is good at spotting predictable, consistent behaviors. Knowing this, you can expand your dog's vocabulary and impress your friends by associating specific spelled-out words with specific actions. She may never hound you for a game of Scrabble, but your dog could "understand" that *t-a-l-k* means you want him to let out a woof and that *r-e-m-o-t-e* means that you want him to fetch the television remote for you.

My three dogs know that either *out* or *o-u-t* means they should rush to the back door to enjoy a romp in our fenced backyard. I have started to say "t-u-o" to tone down their enthusiastic charge toward the door. They look at me in confusion but get the message when I head to the back door. Sigh. I know it will only be a matter of time before they "figure it t-u-o" and I will have to come up with another word. Challenge accepted! 🐾

Paw Prints

Famous comic-strip dogs include Dilbert's sidekick Dogbert, Charlie Brown's beloved Snoopy, and Odie, Garfield's nemesis. Disney dogs have charmed generations, from Goofy and Pluto to Lady and the Tramp to Dalmatians Pongo and Perdita and their many puppies.

NEW DOG: FRIEND OR FOE?

Whenever I meet a new dog, even one belonging to friends, I get a bit nervous. As a child, I was bitten by a neighbor's dog badly enough that I needed stitches. I love animals but always find myself hesitating before greeting a dog for the first time, even a small one. I guess it is hard to shake childhood memories, but I don't want to be unduly afraid or nervous around dogs. What can I look for to determine if the dog is friendly or not? How should I approach a dog I'm meeting for the first time?

I sympathize. When I was a child, a dog bit me. In fact, children far outnumber mail carriers when it comes to being victims of dog bites. It is okay to acknowledge your fear and to be a bit cautious when meeting a dog for the first time. That's being safe and smart.

It may help to know that when dogs are meeting someone for the first time while leashed, they generally have one of five responses that all start with the letter F. They may be friendly, freeze in place, fidget, try to flee, or feel the need to fight. Fortunately, many leashed dogs are friendly and may even rush at you to say hello. It's okay to tell the owner that you feel nervous around dogs and ask that they not let the dog crowd you.

When greeting any dog, especially one you don't know, avoid a head-on stare. Sustained eye contact can be threatening, even to a friendly dog. I call this mistake "doing the doggy De Niro,"

from that famous scene in *Taxi Driver* where Robert De Niro stares menacingly at himself in the mirror and asks, "You talkin' to me?"

Dogs are terrifically adept at detecting our emotional state by reading our body posture and smelling our body chemicals. Try to be relaxed. Take a deep breath in and exhale. Let the dog approach you. Extend the back of your hand slowly to allow the dog the opportunity to sniff you. Do not hover over the dog, pat him on the head, or try to give him a bear hug—these are potentially threatening gestures. Definitely do not pick up a small dog for a cuddle.

To "read" a dog, you must size up the entire body language of the dog, not relying on just one body language cue. Here are some head-to-tail signs to note.

Ears. Challenging or assertive dogs keep their ears erect, tense, and pointed forward. Calm, contented dogs tend to relax their ears. Fearful or worried dogs often pull their ears flat against their heads.

Eyes. Direct staring by a dog means confidence and, possibly, dominance. Dogs who look at you and then look away are indicating that they are yielding power to you. Dogs who greet you with "soft eyes" are content. Large, dilated pupils can be a sign of fear or aggression, especially in conditions when the lighting should make the pupils contract.

Mouth. A soft, relaxed mouth indicates a relaxed dog. A tight mouth or tensed-up lips show tension. A curled lip with exposed teeth often signals aggression, though in some "smiley" breeds such as the Chesapeake Bay retriever, it is a sign of friendliness. Tongue flicking often reveals a feeling of uncertainty or uneasiness.

Yawning usually indicates stress, not fatigue. Yawning helps lower a dog's blood pressure to help him stay calm. Dogs who mouth your hand without using their teeth are delivering a friendly greeting. However, dogs who use their teeth are challenging your authority.

Torso tension. Muscle tension is a good barometer to the emotions a dog conveys. Tightened muscles, especially around the head and shoulders, often indicate that a dog is either scared or might become aggressive if challenged.

Gestures. Play bowing (chest down, front legs extended, back end up, tail wagging) is the universal canine sign for happiness and an invitation to play. Nudging you with a nose is a plea for affection or a cue that you're in his chair and could you please move. Lifting a paw often means "let's play" or "pay attention to me."

Tail. An alert dog holds his tail tall and erect. A fearful dog tucks his tail between his legs. An excited dog hoists his tail high and wags it quickly from side to side. A cautious or nervous dog holds his tail straight out and wags it slowly and steadily. A contented dog keeps his tail relaxed and at ease.

The play bow is understood by all dogs as a friendly invitation to romp, wrestle, and chase.

Fur. A calm dog displays a smooth coat from his shoulders to his hips. A scared or challenged dog often elevates the hairs along his spine (called hackles) to appear larger in size.

When in doubt, accept the most fearful or aggressive signal. If the back end is acting friendly with a wagging tail, but the dog is grimacing and looks tense, assume the most dangerous end is telling the truth. If there is fear in any body language sign, then fear is the answer. Better to be safe and greet that dog from a distance. 🐾

TERRIER TUM-TUM

My husband and I did a lot of research on various breeds before choosing a dog. We decided on a rare breed called Glen of Imaal terrier because of the breed's sturdiness, compact size, and nonshedding coat. We brought home a spirited puppy we named Byline, who is now 8 months old.

As a first-time dog owner, I don't "speak" dog very well. Sometimes, when Byline flops down and goes belly up, he seems to love me giving him belly scratches. Other times, however, he responds to my belly scratches by growling slightly. How can I better understand what Byline is trying to convey to me?

Congratulations on the new addition to your family. I applaud you for taking the time to research the breeds before making a decision about what best suits your lifestyle. As for learning "dog speak," you cannot focus on just one part of a dog's body and expect to accurately interpret what Byline is trying to tell you. You have to look at the whole package and size up the situation.

You also need to take into account the personality traits of terrier breeds. Although there are always exceptions, terriers tend to be bossy and need to know that you are in charge. They heed owners who are clear and consistent in their body and word cues.

Let's discuss that common canine posture: the belly flop. When a dog rolls on his back and exposes his belly, people usually perceive it as a sign of submission. But pay close attention to the dog's posture and muscle tension. A dog who goes into a shoulder roll and stays tucked, with belly up, muscles relaxed, tongue flicking, and eyes looking at you sideways, is usually submissive. These are good, consistent cues to let you know Byline wants his belly rubbed.

But a dog who openly flops on his back with belly exposed and muscles tight, while staring directly at you and perhaps talking or growling slightly, is a confident dog calling the shots and demanding that you pay attention and do what he wants. At 8 months, Byline is at an age when he is trying to determine his ranking in his "pack," that is, in your household. You need to be in charge. If Byline starts to stare and tighten his muscles while you are rubbing his belly, stand up and have him sit for you. When he does, praise him briefly and then walk away. These actions tell Byline that you are the one calling the shots.

For both your sakes, I strongly encourage you to enroll Byline in a basic obedience class taught by a professional trainer who uses positive reinforcement techniques. You will learn how to manage your challenging adolescent, and Byline will learn the doggy manners that he needs for a lifetime of being a good companion. 🐾

LOVES TO LICK

I adore my golden retriever, but she showers me with too much affection. She is constantly licking my face, my hands, even my toes! Why use the bathtub when she's around? How can I tone down her greetings and still let her know I appreciate her?

You have what I call a "Licky Lou" type of dog. When I first adopted Emma, she was a persistent kisser as well! I'm happy to see that you are concerned about not snuffing out her enthusiastic joy for you. That is very important.

First, recognize that your dog is doing what comes naturally. Puppies instinctively lick their mothers' chins and faces in their constant quest for chow. (Hey, these are fast-growing critters!) This behavior is likely related to the practice of wolves and other wild dogs devouring prey before heading back to their litters, rather than dragging a heavy carcass home. When hungry pups lick at their faces, the adults regurgitate the partially digested meal for them.

But face licking goes beyond the need to eat. Puppies are also conveying that they recognize and honor the elevated stature of adult dogs. Pay attention the next time you go to a dog park or other place with friendly dogs. Notice the ones who come up to others, lower their posture a bit, and gently kiss the muzzle of the other dog. It is their way of saying, "Hey, you rule. Now, wanna play chase?"

63

Breed Byte

Owners of basset hounds, bloodhounds, bullmastiffs, and Saint Bernards know to keep plenty of towels on hand. These lovable dogs are major droolers because of their floppy flews (droopy upper lips).

When it comes to licking people, the motivation may be merely a bit of leftover gravy on our chin that draws the attention of our dogs. But the main reason some dogs shower their owners with kisses is what Aretha Franklin sang about: R-E-S-P-E-C-T. Even as they age, many dogs regard their people as leaders of their pack, the two-legger who deserves admiration. Take it as a canine compliment. Your dog is seeking your attention and your approval.

The number of canine kisses depends on a dog's personality. Strong-willed and adventure-seeking dogs tend to dole out kisses less frequently than sociable, happy-to-meet-all dogs who lick to acknowledge that you outrank them. Some breeds, like golden retrievers, are very mouth-oriented and express themselves with a barrage of kisses.

So, how do you stop succumbing to impromptu doggy baths? Forget about pushing your dog away after that first "kiss." Odds are, this action will only motivate her to deliver more licks because she thinks she failed to

communicate her message the first time. Or she may perceive it as a signal to play and heap on more sloppy kisses.

Your best options are to teach your dog the *Kiss* and *Stop* commands. That is what I did with Emma, who is no longer a kissing machine. Your goal is to acknowledge your dog's strong desire to display her feelings toward you while maintaining your rank as top dog. You also need some backup aids, such as chew toys, to offer as appropriate distractions for oral-minded dogs.

To do this, conduct mini training sessions during ideal times, such as when your dog just wakes up, after a long walk, or anytime she is in a calm mood (not when you've just walked in the door!) and you are, too. Allow her to lick your face or hand once and say *Good kiss* and give her a small treat. Repeat a few times.

Now you're ready to teach her the *Stop* command. When she moves toward licking you, put your hand in front of her face like a traffic cop halting cars and say *Stop*. If she doesn't lick, dole out a treat and praise her.

It can be tough to try to bottle the enthusiasm of a tail-wagger happy to see you home after being gone for way-too-many hours, so you also need to teach your dog a more acceptable greeting than a face bath. Teach her to shake paws or perform a trick, such as sitting up or fetching a favorite toy when you come in the door. In time she will learn that the big payoffs—your affection and a tasty treat—occur when she has licked her licking habit. 🐾

LOOK OUT FOR LAUNCHING LAB!

Our very happy 2-year-old Labrador retriever, Nacho, gets a little too excited when she greets people who come to our house. When the doorbell rings, she races to the door. Try as we might, we are unable to stop her from leaping up and putting her front paws on the shoulders of our guests. Nacho weighs 75 pounds and has knocked down several people. What can we do to keep her from jumping up on people? We don't want her to hurt someone.

A leaping Lab can generate as much force as a determined NFL linebacker tackling a quarterback. Although your dog's intentions are friendly, unlike the linebacker's, the results can be the same, with the recipient of the "hit" landing on the ground, hard.

First, you need to understand why Nacho leaps. In the dog world, leaping up and greeting another dog face-to-face is an accepted form of friendly communication. Watch two dogs who are pals play together. They may behave like a couple of stallions with their front paws touching up high as they romp. Many dogs transfer this canine hello to people in a bid for attention.

When our dogs are pups, we often mistakenly encourage them to leap up to greet us. It's hard to resist a cute, 10-pound Lab puppy when she stretches her front paws up to your thigh to say "hi." By reaching down and responding with a hug or a pat on the head, we inadvertently instill in our fast-growing canines that this is an acceptable behavior.

Nacho is not too old to relearn proper doggy greetings toward houseguests and people she meets with you during walks and other outings. Curb the leaping by having a friend help you teach her *Off* and *Sit*. Start by putting Nacho on a head halter and a leash six feet or longer in length. (See page 135 for more about this type of collar.)

Ask your friend to enter your home, without acknowledging the dog in any way. As Nacho races to deliver an airborne "hello," gently but firmly turn the leash so that Nacho must turn her head toward you. Firmly say *Off!* This keeps her feet on the ground and prevents her from touching your friend.

When she stops trying to jump, immediately say *Good off* and give her a treat or praise. Then ask Nacho to *Sit* and have your friend greet her while she remains sitting. Repeat this sequence a few times in a row to help Nacho understand that sitting nicely earns her praise and a tasty reward but jumping gets no reaction. Expand this tutorial by enlisting other friends to come in and wait to greet Nacho until she sits politely.

Once Nacho has mastered the sit on a leash, you can teach her to sit politely on a rug near your door to greet guests. Like most Labs, Nacho sounds like a very social dog. You don't want to snuff out her desire to greet guests, but if you use *Off* and *Sit* consistently, she will be able to welcome visitors without bowling them over. 🐾

WHY ALL THE WHINING?

I recently adopted Gracie, a 4-year-old mixed breed, from my local animal shelter. I'm guessing that she is German shepherd, golden retriever, and perhaps collie. She was found as a stray and was a little underweight. I wanted an adult dog and adopted her because of her gentle, sweet nature. I have had dogs all my life, but Gracie ranks as the whiniest critter I've ever met.

She shadows me around the house and whines all the time. She nudges me. She seems hungry for constant attention. Even when we return from long walks, she whines. I tell her everything is okay. I hug her. Still, she whines. What can I do to curb this whining? I love her very much, but she is driving me crazy!

Even though Gracie's puppyhood and early adult years remain a mystery, you have the opportunity to develop a new whine-free relationship with her. First, have Gracie thoroughly examined by your veterinarian to rule out any possible medical reasons for her whining. She may have an underlying medical condition that is causing her pain. Other types of whines fall into the "I need help" category. She may feel scared when left alone or be trying to tell you that she really, really needs to relieve herself.

Some dogs whine out of sheer excitement, such as when my Kona eyes a squirrel at the base of a tree on our neighborhood walks. It is a sound of frustration at not being able to reach that squirrel that is clearly taunting her.

Then there are what I call the "want" whines. These high-pitched sounds are employed by dogs who realize that making faux pleas brings on plenty of attention and pampering from their pet parents. Just like some children, dogs might whine when they can see a favorite toy that is out of reach. Be careful not to give in to whines in this category. If you cater to her every whimper, you risk creating a pushy, overly dependent dog who expects you to respond whenever she vocalizes or nudges.

One way to reduce whining is to make sure that Gracie receives plenty of exercise each day. Take her on walks lasting at least 20 minutes. Vary the routes. Play with her in the backyard. At home when she starts whining, try to figure out the reason. Respond to the legitimate ones, like the need to go outside to the bathroom or a reminder that it is dinnertime.

But if she whines for whine's sake, walk away. Ignore her. I mean really give her the cold shoulder. That means do not talk to her, look at her, or touch her. When she is quiet and calm, approach her, praise her calmly, and give her a treat.

You need to break the whine cycle, just like parents must do with fussy toddlers. If you don't nip this habit soon, it could develop into a full-blown case of separation anxiety. Once Gracie learns that whining gets her no attention from you, which is the opposite of what she desires, she will realize that being quiet reaps the best rewards. 🐾

TOUCHY TOES

A couple of months ago, I adopted a Pembroke Welsh corgi from a rescue group. Booker is about 18 months old and, from what I understand, was somewhat neglected by his previous family. He is still adjusting to my home and acts timid and tentative. I've taken steps to make him feel at home with a new doggy bed, treats, and lots of toys.

He enjoys being petted, but he doesn't like his toes touched. He quickly pulls his paw from my grasp and tries to retreat. I know I need to keep his nails trimmed, but how can I convince him that I won't hurt his paws?

First, thank you for giving Booker a second chance and a much better home. You're right. He is still adjusting to this new scene and has to build up his confidence and trust in you. Second, many dogs of all breeds and mixes are fussy about having their toes touched, but corgis tend to be among the most toe shy, for reasons that remain mysterious. Years ago, when I adopted Jazz, a corgi puppy, knowledgeable corgi breeders

and trainers quickly alerted me about this touchy toe trait and encouraged me to play with my puppy's toes from day one. Even though Booker is 18 months old, you can still train him to accept paw or toe touching. He may never welcome having his feet handled, but he can learn to tolerate it.

Even though dogs sport very tough paw pads, similar to thick leather soles on shoes, the rest of their foot anatomy was

not designed to be as durable. The area on top and between the toes is especially sensitive to the touch for all dogs, not just corgis, because the area around the toes is packed with nerve endings that alert the brain to any pressure that could possibly cause pain or injury.

In Booker's case, in addition to his breed tendency, it is unlikely that anyone ever handled his paws, given his history. He may also harbor painful memories of bad pedicures. His nails may have been cut too short, causing bleeding and pain. If so, he will be vigilant in trying to protect his toes from future harm.

But as you mention, all dogs need trimmed nails. Overgrown nails can snag on carpet, scratch bare arms and legs, and affect how a dog walks. The trick is to make toe touching a pleasant experience for Booker. To build his trust, start by teaching him to lift his front paw and touch your outstretched hand (hold a treat in your closed fist to encourage him) while you tell him *Shake paws*. Don't grasp his paw at first, just touch it lightly and let it go. Heap on the praise and the treats.

Slowly work up to holding his paw gently for a few seconds and releasing it before he struggles to escape. Once he is comfortable, ask him to shake with his other front paw. Keep sessions brief and remember the treats and praise, because you are helping to build new, happy memories in Booker.

You're ready for phase two. When Booker returns from a long walk and is resting, lightly touch one paw and give it a gentle squeeze. Watch Booker's reaction. If he seems okay, bring out your happy voice and a treat. Proceed with touching a second paw, followed by praise and treats. I recommend that you also give him therapeutic massages that include touching his feet. If he is relaxed from a massage, he should be more tolerant of having you touch his feet.

Phase three calls for bringing out the nail clippers. Purposely leave them in a favorite place, like on the sofa where the two of you hang out or next to his food bowl. When he sniffs the clippers, praise him and hand out a treat. The goal is to get Booker to start viewing the nail clippers as another part of the household furnishings.

Progress to sitting on the sofa with the clippers and a treat in your closed hand. Invite Booker to come up and sniff your hand. Open it slowly, show the clippers, and hand over the treat. When Booker stays, begin squeezing the clippers and tossing treats to get him to associate the sound with a tasty payday.

After a few weeks, begin clipping one paw at a time at first. Give him a high-quality treat (hot dogs or cheese really motivate most dogs!) after each toe. Then stop the grooming session. Do the next paw the next day. Remember the treats. Gradually, you should be able to give Booker a full pedicure in one session. 🐾

NO MORE NIPPING

After my husband of 59 years died, I decided to adopt a puppy. Buddy fills my house with joy and happiness. He gives me companionship and makes me laugh. I also feel safer having him here, especially at night. Unfortunately, Buddy likes to nip my hands and arms to get my attention. He isn't biting aggressively, but his playful nips cause bruises and occasionally his teeth break the skin. My hands and arms are sore. I tried spraying bitter apple on my hands and arms, but Buddy actually likes the taste! What can I do to stop him from being so mouthy?

Sounds like you have one spirited and loyal puppy. Mouthing is a common behavior for puppies who have very

sharp baby teeth that are falling out to make room for adult teeth. Depending on the breed, this teething period and the desperate need to chew to soothe sore gums can last up to a year. I'm not sure what type of dog Buddy is, but a lot of herding dogs, such as border collies, tend to use their mouths when they're playing. They have been bred to herd cattle and sheep by nipping at their heels. Some hunting dogs, like Labrador retrievers, are also particularly mouthy.

Whatever breed he is, the nipping and mouthing are still painful. Most dogs can't stand the taste of bitter apple spray, but there are always exceptions. An effective alternative is breath freshener spray. The minty taste is far from being a canine favorite.

You might also try dabbing your hands and arms with pickle juice, which contains a very sour additive called alum. It keeps the pickles crisp but is also a good dog deterrent, if you can stand the smell yourself!

It is more important, however, to train Buddy not to nip than to rely on repellents. He is bonding with you and needs to know that his nipping hurts. Around 8 to 10 weeks of age, puppies in litters learn about bite inhibition. When one puppy bites too hard, and his sibling yelps, he learns to soften his play bite. So, when Buddy mouths you too roughly, you need to yelp loudly.

In addition, you need to stand up, turn your back on him, and walk slowly away. The message is, "You are not fun right now, and playtime is over." Buddy wants to play with you, and when you

walk away, he will learn that mouthing ends good times.

That said, Buddy is at an age when he needs to chew. When he gets in a mouthy mood, offer him some suitable chew toys as substitutes for your hands and arms. When you play with him, use thick rope toys or rubber tug-of-wars that provide something safe for Buddy to put his mouth around while protecting your hands and arms. Please resist smacking his muzzle or holding his mouth closed, as these punitive tactics can backfire and cause him to bite more, and harder. 🐾

MARATHON BARKER

How can I get my beagle, Jake, to stop barking whenever someone rings my doorbell, knocks on my front door, or walks past my house? A few barks are okay, but Jake barks on and on and at a volume so high that I want to take out my hearing aid so I don't have to hear his noise. When I yell at him to stop, he ignores me and barks even louder.

Some types of dogs are born barkers. The hound breeds, like Jake and his cousins the basset hounds, foxhounds, and bloodhounds, were bred to communicate with their owners during hunts by barking. In addition to their breed histories, some dogs are very territorial. In their minds, your home is their domain to defend. Jake is sounding the alarm and, if we could translate his barks, he is probably saying, "Come quick! Check it out! Friend or foe? What do you want me to do? Now you're yelling, too, so I'd better keep barking!"

As you can see, yelling at Jake to stop barking is futile, because barking dogs interpret our loud vocalizations as our attempt to join in the warning. Your yelling has unintentionally served to reinforce his yapping. You will need to retrain Jake so that he develops a new association with the sound of your doorbell.

Start by ringing your doorbell. When Jake barks, ignore him. Patiently wait for him to stop. After a few seconds of silence, introduce a cue by saying *Hush* and then reward him. Timing is critical—do not reward him until he has been quiet for several seconds. Think like a dog for a moment. If given the options, which would you choose: to keep barking or hush and garner a tasty prize?

Conduct these training sessions several times a day until Jake heeds your *Hush* cue. Make the pauses between his silence and your *Hush* cue longer and longer. Then start saying *Hush* when he is actually barking and reward him when he stops. Remember not to keep repeating that command, though, because it will only reinforce Jake to continue barking.

Paw Prints

The world record for nonstop barking belongs to a cocker spaniel who was officially documented barking 907 times in 10 minutes.

I also have a backup training strategy: diversion. When Jake barks at a passerby, call him to you and reward him for performing a desired behavior, like sitting in front of you for a moment or fetching his favorite toy. For safety reasons, you don't want Jake to behave like a canine mime when someone approaches your home. It is good that he alerts you, but by trying diversionary tactics and rewarding his silences rather than his noise, you will benefit by having a better-behaved Jake who no longer irritates your ears with nonstop yapping.

Why All the Yapping?

Some dogs bark a little, and some dogs bark a lot. In alphabetical order, here are the top 10 breeds known for their gift of gab, according to the American Kennel Club.

- Airedale
- Boston terrier
- Chihuahua
- French bulldog
- Irish setter
- Miniature pinscher
- Norwegian elkhound
- Pekingese
- Schnauzer
- Shetland sheepdog

The top 10 hush-puppy breeds are:

- Afghan hound
- Basenji
- Boxer
- Brittany spaniel
- Bull terrier
- Cocker spaniel
- Greyhound
- Leonberger
- Newfoundland
- Saluki

TALKING TO DEAF DOGS

I just adopted Oliver, a 2-year-old, from a local Dalmatian rescue group. We connected instantly. One big challenge: He is deaf. I've never had a dog who is unable to hear. How can I teach him to listen to me when he can't hear my words? And how can we safely enjoy walks together? I love Oliver and am searching for ways to communicate with him effectively.

I applaud you for adopting Oliver. No dog is perfect, even those with keen hearing. In the past, far too many good dogs were euthanized simply because they were deaf, whether due to a genetic disorder or injury. Dalmatians, Samoyeds, West Highland terriers, and white German shepherds are breeds at risk for deafness. Hearing loss that affects both ears is known as bilateral deafness.

When it comes to training deaf dogs, first realize that no dog speaks English.

Dogs "talk" to each other primarily with nonverbal body language cues. Any noise they make, be it barking, yipping, whining, or growling, is secondary to their unspoken communication through sniffing, facial expression, and posturing.

Second, recognize that just like hearing dogs, deaf dogs learn through consistency and patience. Instead of giving spoken cues to Oliver, you need to use sign language. Many people have learned American Sign Language to train their deaf dogs, and others have developed signs just for dogs.

You can also create your own hand signals to communicate with Oliver. You need to choose gestures that are distinctly individualized to avoid confusion. You don't want your hand signal for *Sit* to be too similar to your gesture for *Come*. You need to get his full attention in order to teach him effectively.

Start by conducting mini training sessions in a distraction-free area such as your living room with only you and Oliver in the room. Train at an optimum time, like right before mealtime when he is hungry. Catch his eye by waving your

Breed Byte

Dalmatian puppies are born pure white. Their trademark black spots pop up as they mature.

hand and alert his body into attention by foot-tapping the floor for good vibrations.

One of the first commands you need to teach Oliver is the *Watch me* signal. While standing in front of Oliver, take a small treat, bring it to his nose, then move the treat up to your eye. When he follows the movement of the treat, clap or give a thumbs-up approval sign, and then hand him the treat. When he responds to *Watch me* consistently, you are ready to introduce other signs. (See also Training Tips, page 208.)

When Oliver masters a sign, give him a treat and use a consistent success signal like a thumbs-up or clap. Don't forget to smile, because Oliver is looking for visual signals. Use treats and progress slowly. Build on each success, and practice patience. Even deaf dogs are capable of learning dozens of signs and recognizing the difference in your request for a ball or the leash.

Years ago, in a dog agility class I took with my husky mix, Chipper, it took me a couple of class sessions before I realized that my classmate's dog, a Sheltie named Alva, was deaf. I just thought that Dale was a quiet, soft-spoken person! But Alva heeded Dale's hand signals and weaved through poles and dashed through tunnels with unspoken delight.

One word of caution with deaf dogs. Please keep Oliver on a four- to six-foot leash whenever you are walking or traveling so you can control his movement and steer him quickly out of any danger. As an added safety measure, indicate on his tag that he is deaf and provide your name and contact information.

To learn more about training deaf dogs and to get step-by-step instructions on hand signals, visit the Deaf Dog Education Action Fund's website. 🐾

EYESIGHT GONE BUT LOVE REMAINS FULLY FOCUSED

Ricky has been a remarkable dog since the day I adopted him. He used to easily spot birds in the tallest branches and leap just at the right moment to catch a ball I threw at him from a distance. However, he is now 8 and been diagnosed with diabetes. Sadly, Ricky developed cataracts and then became blind six months later. How can I help Ricky enjoy his senior years without him being able to see?

A devastating side effect of developing diabetes is that three out of four dogs will go blind quickly. Some dogs are born unable to see, and others lose their sight to cataracts, glaucoma, progressive retinal atrophy, and other conditions.

As a species, dogs are remarkable because of their ability to adapt if they lose a limb or a sense such as hearing or seeing. They don't worry about their limitations or feel sad about what they can't do. They live in the now. Ricky doesn't need to see you to know how much you love him. He already relies more on his keen sense of hearing and superior sense of smell.

Your number-one mission is to ensure that Ricky feels secure and is safe inside your home and on outings. Like you probably did when Ricky was a puppy, you need to doggy-proof each room in your home. You don't need to move your furniture, but you could cushion the corners of low tables so he doesn't hit his head. Add a doggy gate at the top and bottom of any stairs.

To help Ricky find his food and water bowls, place them on a rubber mat if you have tile or hardwood floors so he can pick up that surface distinction. Ricky's sense of smell may be fading as well. Consider adding a strongly scented aroma, such as a dab of vanilla extract near his bowls and at the back door to guide his nose.

Tap into Ricky's hearing prowess. Create good vibrations by having different sounds mean different things. For example, stomp your feet when you want to get his attention quickly. On leashed walks, hum to help him to stay by your side. Reinforce key training words, like *Wait* and *Stop* so you can steer Ricky away from tripping on an uneven sidewalk or stepping into a deep mud puddle.

Most of all, lavish plenty of patience and love on Ricky. He may surprise you with how quickly he adapts when he feels your support. Most of all, embrace every day together. You are blessed to have one very special dog. 🐾

CANINE QUIRKS:
Why Does My Dog Do That?

Sometimes our dogs do wild and crazy things that puzzle us. We wonder why they can't just act more like, well, humans. It would make life so much easier if our dogs would greet people by extending their front paws for a hearty hello, or bypass the toilet and drink fresh water from their bowls, or resist the temptation to raid the cat's litter box for a late-night snack.

Face the Fido facts: Dogs will be dogs. If they could express themselves in words, dogs would probably admit that they are equally puzzled by our behavior. Why, for example, do people fail to sniff others during introductions? Why do people not utter at least one "I mean business" bark when a delivery guy dares to ring the doorbell? And, come on, people, there's a dead fish marinating nicely on the sandy beach—why aren't you rolling in it?

Don't worry. By the time you finish this section, you will possess so much more dog sense that your canine pal might even come up and congratulate you with a big sloppy kiss or a quick sniff of your rear end.

A CASE OF THE ZOOMIES

Sometimes, it seems like a switch turns on inside my dog, Keller. One second, he is lounging on his doggy bed, and the next, he is sprinting down the hallway, bouncing on my bed, and bounding back to the living room only to repeat this speedy circuit several times. What causes him to act this way?

It sounds like Keller has a happy case of the canine zoomies. Don't worry. This sudden burst of energy is perfectly normal in dogs. At least once or twice a week, my Kona will dash outside, pause to look at me, and then start circling the backyard at high speed for two to three laps. Then she stops in front of me with her tail wagging so I can praise her performance.

In the scientific community, zoomies are more formally known as frenetic random activity periods (FRAPs). The topic of doggy zoomies garnered attention when leading veterinary scientists published their findings in a 2020 study in the *Journal of the American Association for Laboratory Animal Science*. In addition to dogs, the researchers studied other species that exhibit this behavior, such as cats, ferrets, rabbits, and even elephants.

What you are witnessing is a burst of bliss. When he shifts into high gear, Keller is having fun, pure and simple. It's perhaps the equivalent of you finding out you won major money from scratching a lottery ticket and doing a little happy dance to express your inner joy.

From your description, the bursts are short. Keller zooms and then calms down. If you can, please quickly grab anything on tabletops that can topple and break. You don't want a broken heirloom or a bloody paw.

It is important to recognize that zoomies are a way for dogs to release nervous energy or excitement, perhaps after holding still to be bathed, or needing to exercise after a long nap. Do not confuse zoomies with a serious medical condition called obsessive compulsive disorder (OCD). Dogs with OCD may chase their tails, follow shadows,

Sniff It Out!

Dogs may not go ho-ho-ho, but they do show amusement. Instead of giggles, they display a distinct rapid panting to convey pleasure and playfulness.

Look for it the next time you play a game of fetch.

excessively mop the floor with their tongues, or snap repetitively at the air as if they are trying to snag a fly. These dogs need specific medications coupled with behavior modifications to manage these episodes.

If your dog is acting strangely, I suggest you record a video of the bizarre behavior and show it to your veterinarian, who can make a diagnosis. 🐾

POOPING WITH FLAIR

My dog, Penny, is a medium-sized mutt, with probably some type of terrier and beagle mixed in. I'm curious about something I've noticed. When she poops in our backyard, she always circles, circles, circles, sniffs, and then squats. But when she poops on a leashed walk, she doesn't circle. Instead, she will poop and then, with great energy and glee, will kick up the grass with her back feet. Why does she seem to have two different potty styles?

Dogs take their potty rituals very seriously. How dogs make "deposits" is influenced by their environment and their dogitude. Penny feels safe in her fenced backyard. She circles to get into the right position to defecate. One explanation stems from behavior observed in wild dogs, who don't have mowed lawns as lavatories. Circling pats down the grass, so when your dog squats, the feces drop to the turf rather than sticking to her tush.

Another explanation is more navigational. Studies suggest that dogs have strong inner compasses. They prefer being aligned north-to-south over west-to-east, and circling gives them a feel for Earth's magnetic pull.

But on a leashed walk, pooping takes on a whole new level of canine-to-canine communication. Dogs rely on leaving scents to communicate with other dogs. Think of these stinky clues as K-9 Wi-Fi that allow dogs to sniff out what's been happening along the way. Even if previous poop has been scooped, other dogs will know about it.

A poop deposit contains a lot of data for other dogs to download, such as

Penny's gender, health status, and even what she had for dinner. But that back leg kicking action releases further scent clues about a dog's social status. Penny is performing "scrape behavior"—using the glands in her paw pads to release pheromones. Interestingly, the scents from the paw pads linger longer than the scent from poop, which explains why your dog's paw pads may stink even if there is no dirt or doo-doo on them. It probably means she has just released her scent from the paw pads.

A few seconds of kicking up grass is normal behavior. However, if Penny starts to kick with more gusto and longer duration, it may be a clue that she is anxious or defensive about some change in her environment. Perhaps she has sniffed out the arrival of a new, potentially aggressive dog in the neighborhood or she's feeling stressed by the loud noises and strange people on the site of the major remodeling going on down the block.

You can keep those paw kicks to a minimum by getting Penny's attention with a treat and getting her to pop into a sit to access this reward. You are shifting her mindset to a preferred behavior—and saving your neighbor's lush lawn. 🐾

Become a Poopologist

One of the most accurate ways to gauge your pet's health is to pay attention to your pet's daily feces deposits. Yes, poop does matter. That's why in my veterinarian-approved pet first aid/CPR classes, I encourage my students to become poopologists.

It may surprise you to learn that veterinarians score the quality of your pet's feces on a scale of 1 to 7. The ideal score is between 3 and 4, meaning the poop is log-shaped, slightly moist, and chocolate brown. To help my students visualize this, I say it should look like a glistening Tootsie Roll.

A score of 1 to 2—meaning the poop resembles little dark rocks, kind of like Milk Duds—could indicate your dog is suffering dehydration and constipation. Very runny stools or diarrhea, which score 6 to 7, might be triggered by spoiled food, stress, or an underlying medical condition.

The color of the poop also offers clues. Healthy poop is chocolate brown. Here is a rundown of red-flag colors of concern.

- **Black** could signal bleeding in the upper gastrointestinal tract.

- **Gray and greasy** could be due to a problem with the pancreas.

- **Green** could be from your pet eating grass, or it might signal a gall bladder problem.

- **Red** in the stool may be blood from ruptured capillaries (tiny blood vessels) in the rectum if your pet overexerts while pooping. Or it could indicate serious internal bleeding. If you see this, don't wait—get your pet to your veterinarian.

- **Orange or yellow** could signal liver issues or an infection in the GI tract.

- **White spots** that look like grains of rice may be tapeworms or other parasites.

One final clue to look for: If you see something that resembles coffee grounds and the poop emits a strong, stinky odor, those "grounds" may actually be dried blood. This may be due to internal bleeding and is a medical emergency that warrants an immediate veterinary visit.

And that's the scoop on your dog's poop!

WHY THE FUSS OVER THE FEDEX GUY?

The postal carrier comes to my house every afternoon and places mail through the slot in my front door. His arrival sets off my dog, Grange, who goes ballistic, barking and lunging at the front door. Grange also launches into a barking barrage when a delivery person rings my doorbell. I'm not winning any popularity contests with my mailman or delivery people. What can I do to get Grange to calm down?

Don't you wish that you could just have a person-to-dog chat with Grange and explain the deal about delivery people? Unfortunately, Grange is abiding by a well-known doggy formula: Dog hears or sees someone in a uniform approach the front door. Dog sounds an alert to the leader of his pack (that's you) and barks aggressively at the intruder. The intruder then retreats, convincing the dog that he has successfully stopped yet another home invasion. The score is always Dog 1, Uniform 0 in this daily delivery game.

Grange may bark out of a need to protect or out of sheer fear, depending on his personality type, but either way, each time this scenario occurs it cements his belief that his actions are working.

It is vital to ensure the safety of these folks in uniform. National statistics indicate that dogs bite some 3,000 postal carriers each year. For starters, there are a couple of things not to do when a delivery person arrives at your front porch. When Grange barks, do not say things like "It's okay" or "Good boy," because that actually rewards him for barking. In his mind, he thinks that you are agreeing with his need to be a ferocious barking machine. At the same time, don't yell at him to shut up—he'll just think you are helping him warn off the intruder.

Here are some things you can do. First, see Marathon Barker, page 72, for some tips on teaching a barker to hush. You mentioned that you have a mail slot. That slot can deliver not only mail but also doggy treats. See if your postal carrier and other delivery people are willing to help by putting treats through the slot. You can keep a sealed container of treats outside your door.

The idea is to get Grange to anticipate good things when the uniformed people approach. (Sure beats junk mail!) This technique is known as counterconditioning. You are striving to replace a bad association with a good one.

If you happen to spot the mail carrier or delivery person coming up the street, you can implement a barking prevention plan. Sprinkle treats on the floor in front of your door for Grange to eat while deliveries are being made.

Timing is important. You must present the treats before he makes his first bark. He cannot be madly barking while gobbling a shower of treats. It's impossible for these two actions to occur at the same time.

Another strategy requires you to clearly step into the role of household commander so that Grange realizes, when a uniformed person approaches, you are the one who calls the shots. If Grange already knows how to sit and greet visitors to your house politely, he can learn to extend that courtesy to people delivering packages. (If not, see Look Out for Launching Lab!, page 65.)

Keep Grange on a leash and ask him to sit while you accept packages in the doorway. Reward him each time he complies. If the delivery person is willing, have them give him a treat.

If the sight of a uniform is too much at first, you may need to fit Grange with a head halter or other device that provides control without pain. (A head halter is a light muzzle that controls the dog's movement by gently turning his head toward the person holding the leash. See page 135 for more information.) If you are not confident about how to put on a head halter, then seek help from your veterinarian or local dog trainer. The ultimate goal is to wean Grange off the halter when he consistently stays in a sit while you accept the delivery.

Instilling proper greeting behavior from the time a dog is first brought home should prevent any barking, snapping, or lunging habits from ever developing. When I brought home my first puppy, I would carry him to the door to meet and greet my delivery people. They would give him a treat and a couple more when he learned to sit on cue. As he grew up, Jazz learned that the person in uniform is like a canine Santa Claus and would happily join me at the front door. He would then plop into a sit and wait for his reward without a single bark. 🐾

CHAMPION CROTCH SNIFFER

This is a bit embarrassing, but I need your help. My friendly and otherwise polite Great Dane greets our guests by rushing up to them and sticking her nose in their crotches. Dolly is a big dog, and it is difficult for me to yank her back. She is good about not jumping up on people, but some of my friends are offended by her preferred method of greeting. What can I do to stop this obnoxious behavior?

Dolly is 100 percent dog. When dogs meet and greet each other, it is very common for them to sniff each other thoroughly from head to tail. The canine nose gives the "sniffer" a lot of details about the "sniffee" (age, health condition, what they ate for breakfast, and even their moods). They aim for the rear end because the scents are more intense there than other parts of the body.

Dogs like Dolly need to learn that this doggy greeting is not well received by the two-legged crowd. Large breeds, like Great Danes, are generally the biggest offenders, because their noses are just the right height to poke someone between the legs. It is not uncommon for them to lean in for both a front and a back sniff. Tiny breeds like Chihuahuas and Yorkshire terriers are more apt to be fascinated by a newcomer's shoes or ankles, because that's as high as they can reach.

Please don't be embarrassed. Plenty of dogs are guilty of this "crime," and people shouldn't get too huffy and offended by what is perfectly polite canine etiquette. You can, however, teach Dolly to be a more acceptable greeter. The goal is to show her the preferred way to say hello while making it worth her while to change her behavior. The first step is to make sure she has a good grounding in basic obedience. All dogs, but especially giant ones like Dolly, need to be taught to sit and stay when told.

Reinforce those commands when the house is quiet, and then have her sit and stay when a guest comes in the door. Ask your guests to approach Dolly, rather than letting Dolly take the initiative.

Some dogs are very expressive with their front legs. If that is the case with Dolly, you can teach her to swap sniffing for paw shaking. Start by working with her by yourself. Ask her to *Sit*. Hold out a treat in your hand, positioned just below her nose. Most dogs will paw at the treat. When Dolly does this, grab her raised paw, shake it in a friendly way, say *Good shake* or *Good paw*, and then hand over the treat. Give her plenty of praise for a job well done.

A modified version of this is the palm sniff greeting. Hold your outstretched hand in a traffic cop "stop" gesture in front of Dolly. As soon as her nose touches your open palm, say *Good greet!* and quickly dole out a treat from your other hand.

Once Dolly is shaking paws or sniffing palms consistently, invite friends to give her the *Good shake* cue. If Dolly slips back to her old routine, ask the guest to simply turn around and walk a few paces away and ignore Dolly. She will soon learn that the sniffing doesn't yield her the goodies that sitting politely

to shake paws does. Work on extending the time Dolly stays in a sit, too.

Finally, expand your horizons by practicing this greeting with Dolly when you are outside the home. Do it when friends approach you during walks or when you are at a dog park. The goal is to expose Dolly to a lot of situations so she learns this is an acceptable greeting for people, as long as they initiate the contact. 🐾

MAKING A SPLASH

I swear that my dog, Jesse, is part duck. He loves to splash water out of his bowl with his front paws. He creates a big mess all over the kitchen floor. The bowl is empty and I keep refilling it, only to have Jesse paw out the water again. What's going on?

Jesse is certainly making a big splash—of the undesired kind. You shouldn't need rubber boots to wade through your kitchen! I'm not sure what breed Jesse is, but he's probably a water-loving breed like a Labrador retriever. These dogs are drawn to swimming and playing in water (and doing the full-body shake afterward).

Every dog-occupied home needs bowls of fresh, clean water to keep canines hydrated. I can see how tricky that might be in your home, but there are several approaches to resolve this watery mess. First, the ever-growing population of pet owners has created a big industry of new pet products. You can purchase water bowls in all shapes, sizes, and structures.

If Jesse is actually knocking over his bowl, you might consider one with a nonskid bottom. A bowl that sits off the ground on a platform might thwart his splashing efforts. You can also consider a water feeder bottle that requires the dog to lick at the tip to release a small flow of water (similar to those used for rabbits).

Another strategy is to monitor your dog's water intake rather than leave water down for him at all times. Present the water bowl half-filled after meals or after Jesse comes in from a long walk or other type of exercise. Put the bowl down and let Jesse drink. If he starts to put his front paws into the bowl, pick it up. Wait for him to sit or become calm and then put the water bowl back down again. You are trying to convey to Jesse that his water bowl is not a source of play but only for quenching thirst. If you opt for this method, be sure you offer him water numerous times throughout the day, especially during hot weather.

Good luck with Jesse, and be sure to keep plenty of paper towels and a mop handy during this transitional time. 🐾

Come On in—the Water's Fine!

If you have a water-loving dog, offer him a suitable outlet to make a splash. Buy a small plastic wading pool for your backyard or patio. Fill it about halfway with water, and let your dog romp and splash outdoors to his heart's content—always under your supervision. Think safety first. As he is getting used to his personal pool, make him feel welcome with praise and an occasional treat tossed into the pool.

LAVATORY LAPPING

I keep several water bowls around my house and always dutifully fill them with clean, fresh water. But Jules, my boxer, prefers lapping water out of the toilet bowl, which I find disgusting! Why does he do that? Will he get sick?

Disgusting is the right description for this doggy deed. But to Jules, the toilet simply provides an oasis of fresh, cool water in a huge bowl that never moves or tips over and is always full. And don't forget about location. Bathrooms often feature tile floors that soothe canine pads on hot days. No wonder Jules views the toilet as your home's number one water bowl.

Another reason Jules may head to the bathroom could be the water bowl you're using. Plastic bowls absorb odors and may cause the water to taste off, even to a dog. Consider switching to ceramic or stainless-steel water bowls that can be easily cleaned in the dishwasher.

It may surprise you to learn that in general the water in your toilet bowl is actually cleaner—and safer—than most puddles, lakes, and ponds. It's a sad fact that these public bodies of water often harbor nasty germs and parasites that can cause giardia and other health conditions in our dogs. Although picking up bacteria from toilet water isn't a big concern, there is a slight risk that your dog could get sick from ingesting cleaning fluids, especially if you use a product that releases chemicals with each flush.

The simplest solution to this problem is to keep the lid down. I know that is easier said than done. We often forget, or visitors leave it up inadvertently. You can put up a discreet sign for guests reading *Please keep the lid down to stop Jules from drinking.* Or you can keep your bathroom door closed.

A final tip: Water bowls kept in sunny places can be doggy turnoffs. Make sure that water bowls are in spots where they will keep cool.

DOING THE DEAD FISH DANCE

My 1-year-old foxhound is in constant search of different smells and always has his nose to the ground. I recognize that is the nature of being a scent breed, but Clyde doesn't just stop at sniffing. Whenever he discovers a rotting frog or fish on the beach or his favorite, roadkill, he takes great delight in flopping down and rolling all over it. He smells horrible afterward. Why on earth does he do this?

No one really knows why dogs roll in smelly stuff, but one theory is that this is an instinctive behavior going back to the time when hunting canines would bring information back to the pack. The thought was, if they found decaying fish, perhaps fresher fish could be found nearby. Some modern-day dogs may have retained this behavior even though it has lost its once-necessary function.

A second theory is that dogs roll in foul-smelling material to provide an olfactory disguise to improve their hunting opportunities. What better way to catch a rabbit, say, than to smell like one, even a dead one, rather than like a dog? This canine camouflage technique also may be employed to hide their doggy scents from other predators.

Unfortunately, dogs and owners will never agree on what smells nice and what smells disgusting. Owners carefully shampoo their dogs, rinse them, towel them dry, and brush them. To them, the dog is finally clean and smelling sweet. To the dog, however, the shampoo is a dreadful stench that needs to be disguised immediately. That explains why many newly bathed dogs will dash outside and roll in the dirt. Some even prefer to roll in poop to cover that awful shampoo smell. It is their version of a high-priced perfume or cologne.

When you are on walks with Clyde, keep him within sight so that you can spot him the minute he dives on a "stink bomb" and distract him from it. If he's found something gross in a particular area, avoid that spot for a few days or leash him until you are safely beyond temptation. Always carry treats with you so that you can call him back to you when he seems too interested in something disgusting.

Reinforce the *Leave it* command so that you stand a greater chance of stopping him before he can roll in the smelly find. (See Ignoring Temptation, page 129.) For people with dogs who roll in droppings, I also recommend stepping up the poop patrol in the backyard to remove that particular temptation.

Breed Byte

The American foxhound dates back to 1650, earning it the distinction of being the oldest American breed.

RAIDER OF THE LITTER BOX

I love dogs and cats and share my home with both. They all get along great, but I can't seem to prevent my dog, Sassy, from eating feces from the litter box. What's the attraction and how can I stop Sassy from these disgusting raids?

You can impress your friends and expand your vocabulary by being able to speak of this behavior by its scientific name: coprophagy (stool eating). The fact that there is a fancy name for this act tells you that Sassy isn't the only canine with this habit, which is shared by many members of the animal kingdom. Many dogs eat the stools of other animals (rabbits, deer, and horses), and some even nibble on their own deposits.

This habit could signal a vitamin deficiency in your dog's diet, so please consult your veterinarian if you suspect that nutrition is involved. Your dog may need to switch to a new diet that is higher in protein, fiber, or fat, or she may need vitamin B supplements.

However, there are other reasons that Sassy partakes in such a revolting habit. When taking care of their young, Sassy's ancestors ingested stools to keep their dens clean and lessen the likelihood of drawing the attention of predators. Nursing bitches still clean up their whelping boxes when their puppies are first born.

A second explanation is a matter of taste. Humans find the idea repulsive, but dogs' palates differ greatly from ours. Litter box stools probably taste of cat food, which most dogs eat happily.

A third reason is that Sassy might be bored and raiding the litter box just to add some zip to her otherwise mundane day. If this is the case, make sure Sassy has two or more regular daily walks of at least 20 minutes so that she uses up some of that extra energy. Spending a few minutes a day teaching her tricks can counter boredom as well. When you leave her alone, provide a distraction to the lure of the litter box by giving her a rawhide bone or a hollow toy stuffed with treats.

Whatever the cause, this problem can be conquered. I recommend that you begin by stepping up your poop patrol and cleaning the litter boxes more frequently. Your cats will also appreciate having their private places—dog-free zones, if you will. In my home, I've placed two litter boxes in a mudroom and blocked the door with a sturdy pressure-mounted gate. It features a hole big enough for my cats to wiggle through but way too small for my big, snack-hunting dog, Bujeau, to even poke her head through.

Blocking access works until you forget to shut the doggy gate to the cat room. Since it's hard to be supervigilant about scooping, you might sprinkle some pancreatic enzymes on the litter when you do scoop. They will make the stool taste anything but doggone great to Sassy. This works only if your cats appear to be unbothered by this addition to their litter box and continue using it. You don't want a sudden litter box boycott by your cats! 🐾

Sniff It Out!

Among the most popular dog tricks, according to many trainers, are *Sit*, *Shake a paw*, *Roll over*, *Speak*, and *Lie down*.

TENNIS, ANYONE?

Every morning when I wake up, I find a dirty tennis ball on my pillow. If I ignore that ball, I get a wet, cold nose in my face and lots of doggy kisses from Nelly, my 1-year-old golden retriever. She is a ball nut. When I take her to the local dog park, she ignores all the other dogs and just focuses on fetching ball after ball. I have to end the game after a half hour because I'm afraid she will run herself to sheer exhaustion. Why is she so consumed with chasing a ball?

Ah, the art and obsession of the ball chase. I see a lot of dogs fitting Nelly's description at the various dog parks in my area. They only have eyes for their favorite toy. When they do come in contact with another dog, they give a quick greeting and go right back to their ball. Some dogs also seem to know which people are the easy marks with the best arms and will use their canine charm to persuade other people to throw the ball when their owner gets tired.

If you think about it, chasing balls isn't that different from chasing rabbits and other small prey. Our dogs' ancestors were the original eat-on-the-run types. The chase brought them a positive prize—food and a full belly. Today, our pampered pooches don't have to pursue their meals, but that chase-and-catch instinct is still wired into the genes of many breeds, particularly hunting breeds like retrievers and spaniels. Even though most family-owned retrievers don't

hunt with their owners, they find that spongy, spit-saturated tennis ball just as satisfying as a downed duck would be. In contrast, you won't find many shih tzus or Akitas begging for marathon ball-tossing sessions. It's just not in their breed history.

Obviously, Nelly is getting plenty of exercise, but it appears that she has crossed the line from being fit to becoming fanatical. The morning ritual also signals to me that Nelly views herself as the one calling the shots—the minute you wake up, she is forcing you to pay attention to her. She is young, but you don't want to run the risk of her developing into a ball bully.

Since you know that the tennis ball motivates Nelly, use it to your advantage in establishing yourself firmly as leader. For starters, put all tennis balls and other similar temptations away at bedtime. Some people stash all balls and Frisbees outside and don't allow any indoor ball play at all. I am in that camp, as my dog Kona loves tennis balls so much that when it's time to come in, she grabs one to drop by the porch door where she can grab it the minute she comes outside again.

Tennis Ball Safety Tip

Not all tennis balls are created equal. The ones discarded at your local tennis courts are too fuzzy for canine teeth. In fact, that fuzz is very abrasive and can wear down your dog's teeth. There's even a term for that—it's called blunting. Blunting exposes tooth pulp. It can make the mouth hurt and make it difficult for your dog to chew his meal.

Protect your dog's mouth by selecting pet-safe, nontoxic tennis balls. Kona is so particular that she will only play with a dog-safe tennis ball brand that contains a squeaker. To avoid any choking incidents, make sure that the tennis ball is not too small for your dog. Fortunately, dog-safe tennis balls come in different sizes— some with that annoying squeaker that Kona loves.

Bring out the tennis ball only when *you* decide it is time to play fetch. With each throw, reinforce Nelly's manners by having her sit and stay for a few seconds or more before you toss the ball again. Use this time to teach Nelly the *Drop it* and *Leave it* cues. (See Ignoring Temptation, page 129.) If she doesn't want to drop or leave the ball, bring out a second ball and offer to throw it if she drops the first one. Work on your recall as well, so that she is paying attention to you and not just the ball during your play sessions.

On those occasions when there are dogs at the dog park who aren't chasing balls, see if you can work on Nelly's dog-to-dog social skills by stashing her toys out of sight temporarily and encouraging her to play some doggy games instead. Or invite a couple of friends with friendly canines over to your backyard or basement for playtime without any toys, especially balls.

I applaud you for knowing when enough is enough and ending the ball-throwing game. Dogs can run themselves into exhaustion by not knowing when to quit, especially in hot weather. Please be sure to provide Nelly with plenty of water afterward. I recommend always keeping a canine water bottle in the car in case the water at the dog park is dirty or your dog doesn't realize she is thirsty until you are back at the car. 🐾

SALAD DAYS

My dog will occasionally eat grass and then vomit a few moments later. He appears fine, and I don't detect any health problem. What's the deal with dogs and grass? I thought they were meat eaters.

Dogs like a little variety in their diet and know the value of adding some greens to the menu. Like humans, they are omnivores, which means they eat meat and vegetation, along with kibble from any available cat bowl (feline food always seems to have a more beckoning aroma), table scraps in your kitchen garbage can (if you forget to close the lid), and all sorts of other things at which people turn up their noses.

Some dogs eat grass frequently and don't throw up afterward. They may simply like the taste and feel the need to add some roughage to their regular meals. This pertains more to those dogs who actually chew and swallow the grass blades thoroughly. Grass also can act as a healthful aid for dogs with upset stomachs who need to purge their systems. In that case, you might notice that they seem to almost gobble the grass without really chewing the blades. The prickly

stalks irritate their stomach linings and cause them to vomit. That sounds like the case with your dog. If this occurs only occasionally, let nature take its course. But if he is vomiting daily and isn't eating well, please consult your veterinarian. There may be an underlying medical reason behind this behavior.

Grass is fine for dogs when it is free of pesticides, lawn chemicals, or other harmful substances. I recommend that you grow a container of grass for your dog to nibble on indoors or provide him with a patch of special greens in your backyard. You will be supplying food that offers certain vitamins and minerals and fiber not found in the meat in his food bowl. And don't forget to entice his taste buds by adding some cooked or raw vegetables, such as green beans or carrots, to his diet. 🐾

THREATENED BY THUNDER

I live in Florida, known as the lightning capital of the country. We have nasty thunderstorms that throw my dog into a four-legged panic. She whines and whimpers when the storms approach and then desperately tries to hide under my bed or in the bathtub. She shivers with fright. Why do thunderstorms cause this strong reaction? How can I help her calm down?

Sadly, your dog is not alone. Even before that first thunder boom or lightning flash, many dogs scurry into closets, crawl under beds, or leap into bathtubs. Dogs in extreme states of anxiety may vocalize, have accidents, and try desperately to hide or to escape what they regard as a house of horrors.

Some dig through carpeting or crash through windows or doors to elude the terrifying noise.

While fear is a normal emotional response to a real or perceived threat, it can escalate to a phobia, an exaggerated and irrational response that can emotionally cripple a dog. Veterinarians and animal behaviorists use the term *noise phobia* to describe the intense and irrational fear displayed by some dogs to certain sounds.

Noise phobia in dogs is more common than you may realize. Though no extensive studies have been done on the number of dogs with phobias of particular sounds, experts estimate that close to 50 percent of dogs demonstrate some signs of fear and anxiety to certain sounds. The list of top canine noise phobias includes thunderstorms, fireworks, backfiring trucks, gunshots, yelling people, squawking pet parrots, and blaring security alarms and smoke detectors. Some dogs develop a phobia of more unusual sounds based on experience, such as the wheels of a skateboard, the buzzer on a TV game show, or the popping of bubble wrap.

While there is no cure or one-size-fits-all solution to minimize a noise phobia your dog has or even make it disappear, you do have plenty of tools at your disposal. Keep in mind that behavior modification techniques build on small but steady successes, and you need

Signs of a Terrified Dog

A dog with a phobia may display these behaviors:

- Inappropriate chewing (your shoes, the television remote, etc.)
- Drooling
- Excessive barking
- Diarrhea and vomiting
- Digging (including the living room rug)
- Panting and salivating heavily
- Pacing frantically
- Trembling and shaking
- Displaying "whale eye"—a panicky look in which you can see the whites of the eyes
- Freezing in one place and refusing to move
- Attempting to flee or escape
- Hiding

to be patient. If the following tips don't work, it may be necessary to consult a professional dog behaviorist or dog trainer to help modify your dog's behavior. Some dogs require prescription medication to help them cope with noise phobias, especially to thunderstorms.

I live in Dallas, where the weather can be wicked. Our Bujeau, a sweet, 90-pound Bernese mountain dog mix, used to be terrified by thunder and lightning and would try to squeeze under the bed or sit on my spouse while drooling and panting excessively. As a certified Fear Free Pets professional, I learned techniques to calm down Bujeau's thundering panic attacks, and you can use these tips to help your dog, too.

In addition to implementing the following strategies, I teamed up with my veterinarian to find a medication that would help take the edge off Bujeau's fear. Now when a thunderstorm is predicted, I give her a dose of her calming medication. I turn on the bathroom fans and the sound machine in the bedroom. I usher her into our windowless walk-in closet, where there is a cushy doggy bed in the corner. Talking to her in a calm, can-do voice, I sit with her and gently stroke her ears. I play music at medium to high volume or watch a show on my laptop as an additional distraction.

Always strive to be calm around your dog, and avoid baby talk or panicky tones. Dogs are masters at reading our emotional states. High-pitched or rapid speech will only make your dog feel that you are also scared.

For some dogs, an antianxiety vest or antistatic jacket can help them feel less anxious or frightened. Even wrapping your dog in a large towel can have a calming effect. Another trick to try is to rub unscented dryer sheets over your dog's head and back. More than the noise of thunder, some dogs become agitated by the buildup of static that occurs in an electrical storm, and the dryer sheets help dispel static.

You can also experiment with pheromone sprays and diffusers that emit dog-appeasing scents; these help some dogs calm down in stressful or scary situations. 🐾

ATTACKING TOYS WITH DOGGED DETERMINATION

Why does my dog take such delight in attacking soft plush toys and ripping out the stuffing? Are there any safety concerns?

You troll the aisles of your favorite pet supply store in search of what you deem to be the most perfect stuffed plush toy for your dog. You come home and hold the new toy up for your dog. Before your very eyes, your sweet canine transforms into a focused hunter the second you playfully squeeze the toy a few times to trigger the high-pitched squeaker within.

In a matter of minutes, your living room is littered with stuffing. That toy never really had a chance. Despite the fact that dogs have been domesticated for thousands of years, many of them have never lost their hunting instinct.

Though we provide them with plenty of good food and healthy treats, most dogs need—and want—to hone their hunting skills. Lacking access to real prey, dogs love to stalk and "kill" pretend prey. Terrier, sporting, and hunting breeds lead the pack when it comes to gutting stuffed toys. Some dogs delight in using their teeth to surgically open the toy and toss out the stuffing in order to retrieve the squeaker. Think of this as the canine equivalent of finding the prize in a box of Cracker Jack.

For dogs who are extremely bored or anxious and need something to do, chewing is a favorite way to pass the time or soothe frayed nerves. Gutting a toy gives dogs a sense of accomplishment. It also serves as an outlet for excess energy.

You can increase the challenge by wrapping the plush toy in an old T-shirt and tying the ends off. Replacing plush toys can be pricey, so consider offering your dog more durable toys, such as hollow, hard rubber ones.

Finally, always supervise play with plush toys and immediately clean up the stuffing. In your dog's haste to gut a toy, he may swallow the squeaker or stuffing. That can cause stomach or small intestinal blockages and require surgery. Take your dog to the veterinary clinic immediately if he seems to have abdominal pain, drools, lacks an appetite, acts lethargic, or is vomiting after tearing up a plush toy. 🐾

STARES AT STAIRS

My terrier mix, Danny, is a very confident fellow. He boldly goes up to larger dogs at the dog park and solicits them to play. He doesn't blink during thunderstorms and loves to greet visitors to my home. The problem is that I have recently moved to a condominium on the second floor with outside stairs. Danny dashes up the stairs when we come home, but when we are going out, he freezes at the top of the stairs and I have to pick him up and carry him down. What happened to his confidence?

There are a number of reasons for dogs not wanting to tackle stairs, even enclosed ones. Danny's reluctance could be due to a medical condition, such as arthritis or hip dysplasia, so have that possibility checked out first. A key clue in this particular canine mystery is that outdoor stairs are often open, without solid risers between the steps. Danny is no dummy. To him, these stairs give him glimpses of the pavement far below, a vision as inviting as peering over the edge of a cliff.

Many dogs easily run up a flight of stairs but find the prospect of heading back down intimidating because they are less stable going down and more likely to slip or overbalance. Some dogs try to avoid stairs at all costs because of memories of a spill. Who wants to repeat that scary scenario?

It is tempting to give in to those pleading eyes and to offer him some soothing words and carry him down the stairs. But the problem with these actions is that they can unintentionally foster apprehension in our dogs and cause them to be even more fearful. Forget trying to scold Danny, either. Bullying him to go down the stairs solo without addressing his fear will only generate more behavior problems and weaken your relationship.

Instead, take it literally one step at a time with food bribes. Some of my favorite dog trainers recommend placing a mediocre treat (an ordinary dog biscuit) on the first step and then an irresistible treat (a piece of chicken breast or bacon) on the next step. Without saying a word or giving any nudges, let Danny scope out the situation with his nose and his eyes. Once he is brave enough to touch the stair with his paws, or even conquer one step to get the premium treat, heap on the praise like he won an Oscar.

You won't be able to get Danny to be a stair champion, descending swiftly after one training session. Work a few minutes each day to expand his comfort level by placing the best treats on steps farther and farther down. During this transition when you are still toting him down the stairs, try whistling or singing a happy tune while striding confidently down the stairs. Danny may pick up on your mood and decide that the stairs are not so scary after all. 🐾

SKIDDING TO A STOP

We just replaced the carpet in our home with what we thought would be more pet-friendly tile and laminate flooring. These smooth surfaces are much easier to keep clean and clear of pet hair, but Kelsey, our golden retriever, took a spill after turning a corner too fast while chasing a tennis ball with our teenage son. Now she is afraid of the footing and walks gingerly around the house. How can we restore Kelsey's confidence so she doesn't slink around the house?

Your floors are pet friendly in that they are easy to clean, but they lack the traction that dogs need to move confidently around the dining room table and through the family room. Barring any physical injury, the spill probably made Kelsey feel a bit like Bambi on ice with legs splaying in all directions.

To help her feel steady on her feet again, the first thing you should do, not only to increase her confidence but to make it safer for her, is to strategically place rugs with nonskid backing around doorways, in hallways, and in the center of larger rooms to give Kelsey better traction when navigating around the house.

Secondly, I recommend that your son and your dog take those fun chasing and ball-tossing games outside. The idea is to teach her that the house is a calm place with food goodies and outside is where the spirited fun happens. Have everyone in the family speak to Kelsey with "library" voices inside the house and reserve loud, excited tones for outdoors. Slow things down inside, including your body language. For example, when you feed her, put her bowl down gently. When you call her to come to you, do so quietly, without expecting her to bounce up to you. Your actions will give Kelsey the idea that she can relax in her home.

It's also important to give Kelsey a suitable outlet to unleash her need for speed. Make sure she is getting enough exercise so that she doesn't have excess energy to burn inside. Convert casual strolls around the block into walks that cover more ground at a faster pace. Play fetch with her or treat her to playtime at a doggy day care or dog park. When she comes back home, she will be a tired and happy dog who is less apt to want to dash around indoors.

Finally, reinforce the *Sit*, *Stay*, and *Lie down* cues so that when you wash the floors or have to clean up a spill, you can adequately control Kelsey's movement while you thoroughly dry your floor. 🐾

CONFERENCE CALL INTERRUPTER

I work primarily from home and often communicate with my staff and clients via video calls. The problem is that Felix, my Yorkie mix, pesters me whenever I am on an onscreen meeting. He barks, yips, tries to jump in my lap, and brings toys for me to toss. I need to be professional. How do I get him to leave me alone?

Put yourself in your dog's place for a moment. As far as Felix can see, there is no one else in the room, but you're vocalizing. Naturally, he thinks you're talking to him. But when he responds, you ignore him, so he persists in trying to get your attention. If you do respond, in an effort to make him settle down, you are actually rewarding his irritating behavior. Unchecked attention-seeking behaviors can develop into serious behavior problems. Forcing you to pay attention to him gives your dog the wrong idea about who is the real leader in the house.

It's time for a workplace intervention. As cute as Felix may be, he needs

to be in a crate or another enclosed area with his doggy amenities while you conduct important work meetings. Teach him that crate is great. I view crates as welcoming canine condos. Most dogs like to den up in a place that feels cozy and safe. Provide him with comfy bedding to encourage him to take catnaps. Up the real estate value of his crate by periodically tossing in treats for him to chew.

Perhaps the most effective technique in the long run is to extinguish the behavior by completely ignoring Felix when you are on the computer. In the beginning, practice by arranging a pet-loving friend to join you in a practice video call. Remain standing to keep Felix from jumping up or depositing toys in your lap. Turn your back on him, and do not look at him or speak to him. Be prepared for his annoying behavior to increase at first, as he will work harder to get your attention.

It takes time for the cold-shoulder routine to work and for your dog to start realizing that his actions don't generate any attention from you, good or bad. When he leaves you alone and after you end your call, go over to him calmly and tell him *Good settle*, and give him a treat for being a well-mannered dog. And be glad Felix is not pestering you for his own online account! 🐾

BURIED TREASURES

Why does my dog seem so interested in burying his bones and even some of his favorite stuffed animal toys in the backyard? Even worse, he sometimes goes out the dog door, digs them up, and brings the muddy mess back inside the house—always smiling and wagging his tail.

Doggy doors have their benefits and their downsides. No one likes to come home and find muddy paw prints and smears from unburied canine treasures all over the floors.

Before they joined our households as pets, dogs did not know where their next meal would come from, so after a kill they would bury any uneaten food to hide it from scavengers. When they were hungry again, they would return to their cache and dig up their leftovers. The dirt also helped keep their food fresher longer by protecting it from sunlight.

Your dog is just following that ancestral call to hide his food. Even though you feed him every day, you can't take that "must stash food for a hungry day" mentality out of him. The same goes for those extra toys he stashes away. Be glad he doesn't take other household items like the TV remote or your wallet—both have been known to happen!

Keep in mind that dogs tend to bury extras, not essentials. Patrol your house and pick up any spare dog bones or toys. Limit his access to one bone and one toy at a time. Vary the type of dog bones and toys from time to time to keep him interested. By limiting the quantity and providing variety, you may lessen his motivation to take his treasures out to the backyard.

Make his favorite digging spots less attractive by covering them with chicken wire or bricks or other objects that are not paw friendly. And try offering your dog a less-destructive indoor option: Show him how he can bury his favorite bone or toy under a blanket instead. 🐾

GETTING OVER THE HUMP

Rocky, my boxer, is neutered, but that doesn't seem to matter to him. When visitors come over, Rocky runs up to greet and sniff and then tries to hump their legs. I am so embarrassed. Why does he do this, and how can I break him of this bad habit?

Although intact male dogs are the most frequent offenders, neutered males and even spayed females are capable of humping legs and other objects. While it is usually viewed as a sexual action, some dogs mount as a form of play or when overexcited and unsure of the correct behavior. In your case, humping may be the way Rocky is alerting new guests that he is a powerful pooch.

In neutered males and spayed females, humping signifies a bit of bullying and daring to push the boundaries. Your dog is challenging you and others to see how far he can assert himself with humans. It is vital to stop this habit before it escalates to more aggressive types of behavior. If your dog gets away with humping, he may begin growling and air-snapping at guests.

The peak time for this behavior to surface is during the challenging teen years, which in dogs equate to between 6 months and 2 years old, depending on the specific breed. The smaller the dog, in general, the faster the maturation. In Rocky's case, his physical strength and size might be spurring him on to continue humping since he can get away with it. He needs to learn that you are the leader of his pack and that guests also outrank him.

Breaking your dog of this habit will take time and patience. Start by making Rocky work for his needs and desires so that he understands that he has been demoted. He must sit to greet people, lie down and wait before receiving his food bowl, and wait at doorways for people to go through before him. (See Paying the Price, page 124.)

To show Rocky what is acceptable behavior, put him on a leash when he is greeting people, and make him sit and wait for them to come to him. Step on the leash and sharply tell him "stop it" when he starts showing too much interest in their legs. If his behavior persists, discuss with your veterinarian the possibility of temporarily using an antianxiety medication as an adjunct measure to let some air out of his Big Dog ego and to chill his libido.

You don't mention if Rocky acts this way with other dogs, but I see humping at dog parks far too much. Size doesn't seem to matter, and sometimes the humping dog is smaller than the object of his mounting. A dog may mount another dog because he is confused about how to act when first meeting new dogs. Mounting is also an assertive way to show who ranks as top dog, literally. The "humper's" victory over the "humpee" is a way that dogs in the wild determine without fighting who earns the right to procreate with the best available bitches in the pack.

You can't always stop another person's dog from humping your dog, but you can teach your dog some defensive postures that may curb the mount-minded canine. If possible, get your dog to sit. A sitting dog is less easy to hump than a standing one. You can also call your dog over to you. If possible, use your body to block access to your dog. Try to distract the other dog by tossing a tennis ball in the opposite direction. 🐾

MUTT-SEE TV

I have three dogs. Two of them pay close attention to the actions and the sounds on my television. The third pays no heed. What kind of TV do some dogs like?

Welcome to the world of the twenty-first-century dog. Improved television technology has made images lifelike, and the audio quality is far superior to that of even a few years ago. The short answer is that dogs, just like people, have personal preferences. Like yours, my three dogs have very different reactions to onscreen activity. Kona, a terrier mix, will go sniff the television if a dog pops into view, big Bujeau will look up but stays on the sofa, and little Emma pays no attention at all, even to barking dogs or meowing cats.

I'd be curious to know if your two watchers are also terriers, because one thing we do know about canines and television watching is that terriers may be more apt to pay attention to onscreen images. This is probably because they are more hard-wired to look for and chase moving prey than, say, hound breeds that rely more on their sense of smell.

With the advances in technology from the fuzzy, flickering images on old analog televisions to modern high-definition flat screens, it's no wonder more dogs are paying attention to what's playing, especially if there are canines or other animals involved. Some dogs even go crazy for the smaller but still sharp images on a laptop, tablet, or even smartphone.

Your curious canines might enjoy watching a dog-themed movie or a dog show or agility event. There's even a cable channel, DOGTV, dedicated to programming to entertain and engage left-at-home dogs. I enjoyed interviewing DOGTV creator Ron Levi, who works with veterinarians and behaviorists to craft content for the shows. Not surprisingly, they've discovered that dogs stay calmer with more relaxed programming, such as sweeping panoramic landscapes rather than screens filled with barking dogs, which tend to get them all riled up.

Ron is also alert to the fact that dogs see yellow and blue more than other colors (see Seeing Eye to Eye, page 15) and

Paw Prints

Since Eric Knight introduced her in his 1940 novel *Lassie Come Home*, this smart, spunky collie has starred in dozens of books and children's stories. The first film of the original novel, made in 1943, was followed by at least 20 more movies, including a 2001 manga version, and numerous television shows. In spite of her name, Lassie has always been portrayed by male dogs.

makes sure to film in contrasting colors. That means no red balls being tossed against green grass! Color is edited to benefit that dichromatic vision. DOGTV also takes care to provide sounds and music that are soothing, not irritating, to a dog's sensitive hearing.

It's nice that watching television is one more activity that you and your dogs can enjoy together. The goal of DOGTV is to make dogs feel safe and comfortable when they are home alone, but Ron and I agree that it is not a replacement for exercise or a cure for separation anxiety. 🐾

A TAIL'S TALE

Often when my dog wakes up from a nap, he will start circling around to chase after his tail. He seems very determined to catch his tail. He spins around and around and seems almost frantic. I found it amusing at first, but now it's a little disconcerting. Why does he do this?

Researchers do not know why dogs chase their tails but offer the theory that as predators, dogs instinctively react to movement. The blurry movement of a tail may be mistaken for a squirrel or rabbit, and then the chase is on—in circles. Even tail-less dogs will romp around in circles on occasion. As long as the circling is infrequent and stops within a few seconds, chalk it up to one of those weird but harmless canine behaviors.

For the occasional tail chaser, the reason may be as simple as a way to

break up the monotony of a ho-hum afternoon. In mild forms, it can be the canine equivalent of people who twirl their hair, tap their feet, or smack their chewing gum to relieve tension. Some dogs seem to chase their tails to unleash bottled-up energy after being cooped up in a crate for a few hours or, like your dog, after a long nap. Tail chasing offers a quick, easy way to get their muscles moving and their blood flowing.

Some dogs discover that tail chasing rewards them by attracting attention. If you react by laughing, applauding, or offering treats, your dog quickly learns this is a good way to catch your eye and increase the handouts.

Some dogs, however, become tail-chasing addicts out of feelings of anxiety in stressful situations or because of a compulsive condition that requires professional help—and medication—from your veterinarian. If your dog's behavior persists for more than a moment after a nap, or you notice him grabbing at his tail, distract him with a favorite toy or treat. Give him a more acceptable behavior to perform like fetching a ball or Frisbee or joining you on a long, brisk walk in a place with lots of great scents to sniff.

Without intervention, a chronic tail chaser risks injury. Some dogs actually catch their tails and can hurt themselves by pulling and biting them. In extreme cases, these dogs may not stop even to eat or to play with another dog. They literally spin so much that they collapse in exhaustion. Bull terriers and German shepherds seem to be more genetically predisposed to tail chasing.

Please do not encourage your dog to chase his tail or tease him by encouraging him to follow the circular motions of a laser penlight. He may start to perform the same compulsive actions with moving shadows. 🐾

SCRATCHING AND SCRAPING AT THE SOFA

Usually when she settles down for a nap, Maizie, my 11-year-old mixed-breed dog, does the classic "turn around a few times before lying down" move. Sometimes she starts digging at the sofa and won't stop until she has made a big mess out of the slipcover. If there is a blanket on the floor, she paws and scratches at it and even uses her nose and teeth to drag it around like a nest.

Once in a while, she will rumple up the runner in the hallway and then leave it there and go sleep somewhere else. Sometimes she digs and bites at her bed so much that it gets all lumpy and then she doesn't want to lie on it! It sometimes seems like she is more interested in trampling and digging than snoozing. Why does she do this?

Your furniture-remodeling canine is tapping into her ancient canine heritage when she circles, digs, and tramples. Well before the invention of sofas and blankets, dogs in the wild had to sleep in the open if they weren't near a den. At bedtime, Maizie's ancestors huddled together for warmth and protection. Circling provided room for all to stake out a territory while remaining close.

To protect themselves, they dug into the ground and trampled down the grass and other vegetation to make a nest far bigger than they needed. The reason?

They wanted to project the idea that they were bigger than their actual size as a way to fool possible predators. If these nesting areas appeared large, the predator might decide to go elsewhere and hunt for a smaller, more vulnerable target.

Since she doesn't need to make a safe nest, Maizie's pawing and digging at blankets on the floor or rumpling the hallway runner is probably her way of making those items more comfortable for napping, just as many humans fuss with our pillows and blankets to make them feel just right before we can sleep. After all her efforts to flatten them out or fluff them up, she may decide that they just won't work out as a makeshift bed, so she leaves the scene in search of a more suitable spot for snoozing. 🐾

PASS THE PLASTIC, PLEASE

Snickers, my yellow Labrador retriever, loves chewing on her plastic food bowl and anything within reach in our house that is made from plastic, such as soda bottles and storage bins. She is about 9 months old. I'm worried that she will swallow bits of plastic and choke. I also want to stop this habit so that more household items don't get destroyed. Why does she do this and how can I stop her?

When it comes to Labrador retrievers, my veterinarian friend Marty Becker is fond of sharing this quote: "Labs chew till they're 2 and shed till they're dead." By this age, most puppies have finished teething, but your Lab is a natural-born chewer who still needs something to work her jaws. Snickers cannot distinguish a dog chew toy from the TV remote. She is on a constant quest to find something, anything, to chew.

First of all, any household with a puppy must be thoroughly puppy-proofed so that tempting objects are out of sight and reach, and access is restricted to certain rooms. Young dogs, especially breeds like Labs, will occasionally nibble on shoes or try a taste test on the corner of your end table. It's part of the normal stage of growing up and exploring the environment.

Snickers needs a suitable focus for her oral fixation such as beef- or chicken-flavored chew bones or hollow toys—made of very durable, dog-resistant rubber—that can be stuffed with treats. Chew toys come in an array of sizes, shapes, and textures.

Make sure you provide her with items that are specifically meant for chewing rather than playing.

Snickers sounds like a good candidate for crate training so that you can control her environment when you can't actively supervise her. Regular exercise every day should also help curb her urge for inedible items. An easy, quick solution is to replace her plastic food and water bowls with ones made of ceramic or stainless steel. These materials are easy to clean but hard to chew and won't retain the scent of food the way plastic does.

Spray bitter apple or sprinkle cayenne pepper on the objects of Snickers's attention, if they are things that can't be put out of her reach. If she does pick up an inappropriate object in her mouth, startle her by clapping your hands or making a loud noise and saying *Leave it!* Reinforce the *Leave it* command by immediately presenting her with a more suitable object to mouth and heaping on the praise. The idea is to stop her from chewing on the wrong items by rewarding her for chewing the right items. (See Ignoring Temptation, page 129.)

Please do not resort to scolding her or grabbing her by the scruff of the neck. These punishments won't help her understand what you want, but they may cause her to become anxious and lose trust in you. 🐾

Pick a Pica Problem

Dogs who constantly seek out plastic and other non-edible materials to chew may be suffering from a condition known as pica. This is usually a psychological rather than a nutritional problem and can result in dogs eating gravel, rubber bands, wool socks, wooden baseboards, and even metal. Not only can these items damage dogs' teeth, but they can also cause intestinal blockages that require surgery.

If your dog regularly eats items that are not part of his normal diet, consult your veterinarian for possible solutions. This is definitely a problem that needs attention.

Righting
DOGGY
WRONGS

Puppies and dogs don't enter our lives with owner's manuals that explain how to instill good manners and avoid undesirable behaviors. In many cases, new owners think their new dog should behave just "because he loves me." Unfortunately, part of the reason behind our constant litany of *No! Bad dog! Drop it! Down! Bad, bad dog!* is poor pet parenting on our part.

After all, dogs take their cues from what we say, how we say it, and what we do. They are not trying to misbehave; they just don't know what the rules are and how they fit in the family. It is our job to explain those things to them.

This section addresses some of the most common challenges I've heard from frustrated owners. Take heart—you're in good company. Even professional dog trainers and animal behaviorists have their share of trying tales, but with consistency, persistence, and kindness, you can convert a canine who is driving you crazy into a dog who is a sheer delight.

LEARNING TO SHARE

We recently adopted a second shelter dog. The two get along fine most of the time, until the new dog attempts to play with a toy belonging to our first dog. She growls and lunges at him—a behavior we've never seen her exhibit. Why won't she let him play with her dog toys, and what can we do about it?

Your first dog has enjoyed her starring role as the one and only, but now she needs to learn a new concept: sharing. Just like humans, dogs give value to certain objects and opportunities in their world. With the arrival of a new dog, your resident dog feels a heightened need to guard and protect what she per-ceives to be her most prized resources: her toys.

It sounds like both dogs need more time to adjust to being "siblings," so feed them separately for a while to reduce the tension. To create a safer and more even playing field, scoop up all the dog toys in your house and place them in a dog-proof container with a lid (use an opaque bin that the dogs can't see through).

Next, institute new dog play rules and reinforce your role as respected leader by starting and stopping all playing time. Dogs are very hierarchal and need to know their rank in the family. Devote 10 to 15 minutes of supervised interactive play with each one separately. Keep one dog in a closed room when you play with the other, and then switch.

When you notice that the two dogs seem to be getting along consistently—maybe napping near each other or romping nicely in the yard—you may be ready to introduce them to playing with toys together. Initially, play it safe by keeping them on long leads. Bring them into a large space. Ask each dog to *Sit* and *Stay* as you hand each a toy.

If one tries to steal the other's toy or lunges, step on the lead and get the dog to sit. Pick up the toys and declare *Game over* as you put them in the toy bin and walk away. You are conveying that good times end when such behavior occurs. When the dogs are playing nicely in the same room, reinforce with praise and healthy treats.

If your first dog seems overly attached to a particular toy, discard it and replace it with two identical new ones. Mark one with an "X." Then purposely mix up which one you gave to which dog during playtime so that their scents (and saliva) can be on both, diminishing the "mine, mine, all mine" attitude.

A final note: It wouldn't hurt to enroll the pair in a basic obedience class taught by a positive reinforcement trainer. Even if your first dog aced the class before, a refresher can't hurt.

Let the (safe) games begin!

TAKE A CHILL PILL, FIDO

My dog turns into a panic puddle whenever we need to take him to the veterinary clinic. He seems to sense the destination during the car ride and goes crazy. What can I do to calm him down?

Fortunately, we are learning more about how to instill a feeling of safety and calmness in our frenzied four-legged friends. It begins with understanding that dogs are more astute about their trusted people's emotional states than many people realize. It's a good bet that before you take your dog to the veterinary clinic, you may feel a bit apprehensive, a little frustrated, or just worried that your dog is going to struggle and exhibit signs of fear, anxiety, and stress.

Don't get impatient and push or force your dog into a carrier or yell at him out of frustration when putting him in your vehicle. Instead, be as gentle as you would putting a baby in a car seat, and say to your dog in a confident tone, "I got this."

At least 10 minutes before the trip, spray your dog's carrier and the inside of your vehicle with Adaptil, which contains canine pheromones that help calm some dogs. In the short term, consult your veterinarian about possibly giving your dog calming supplements ahead of your visit to help reduce emotional stress. Some choices to discuss with your veterinarian are Zylkene and Composure Pro, or medications such as trazodone or gabapentin that may help reduce emotional stress.

Fear Free Handling

My pal Dr. Marty Becker is known as "America's Veterinarian" from his long stint as resident veterinary contributor on *Good Morning America*. In 2016, he founded Fear Free to help all who love pets to prevent and alleviate stress, anxiety, and fear in pets. The organization provides online training and certification to pet parents and professionals, from veterinarians and veterinary technicians to shelter workers and groomers.

As a certified Fear Free professional, I encourage you to investigate, learn more, and seek out certified veterinarians, pet sitters, and other professionals.

When you arrive at your destination, avoid waiting in a crowded lobby. Tell the staff you have an anxious or fearful dog, and arrange to stay in your vehicle with your pet in the parking lot until an exam room is ready.

To help in the longer term, ask if you can make some trial runs with your dog to build up a positive association with the clinic. Call to check if the clinic lobby is quiet, then bring your dog inside for the receptionist to greet and hand a treat. Then leave. If you can do this a few times, you may reduce the level of anxiety that your dog (and perhaps you!) are feeling.

The bottom line is that your dog needs and deserves to be regularly examined by a veterinarian to keep him healthy. Make sure you stay calm while putting your dog in the car, driving to the clinic, waiting inside, and going home. And remember, you got this! 🐾

FEAR FREE
Taking the pet out of petrified.

PUPPY-CLASS CLOWN

My new puppy and I just enrolled in a puppy obedience class, but we're not exactly wowing the trainer or winning over classmates. Happy, aptly named, gets so excited in class that I sometimes lose my grip on her leash and she is off playing with another puppy, trying to steal treats, and jumping in people's laps. I think we're going to flunk the class. Any advice on how I can gain control of this bundle of energy?

First, kudos for enrolling Happy in a puppy class. It is essential for all pups and newly adopted adult dogs to become students in a reward-based obedience class. These classes do more than just teach your dog to sit or stay. They provide an ideal venue for you to bond with your dog, to expose your pup to other dogs and people, and to learn the rules of canine etiquette. Some dogs are visual learners—puppy see, puppy

do—so watching canine classmates being rewarded for appropriate behaviors may be a good incentive.

Don't worry; you and Happy will not become puppy-school dropouts. Remember that, as with all youngsters, a lot is going on both mentally and physically inside your personality-plus pooch. She is easily distracted and has no impulse control, so your job is to provide limits for her behavior until she begins to understand what her role is. Here are some insider secrets to achieve puppy-school success (and a diploma).

Take Happy for a brisk 20- to 30-minute walk before arriving at your class. That way, she will have unleashed some of her pent-up energy and excitement.

Arrive 5 to 10 minutes early to allow your puppy to satisfy her uncontrollable need to meet and greet other classmates (both people and other puppies) and to relieve herself. Many puppy classes have socializing as part of the lesson plan. For those that do not, this "play preview" can help Happy work through her excitement.

Don't feed her before class. Depending on the time of the class, wait to serve up dinner until after the class or feed her only a half portion, saving the rest for later. Hungry puppies are more motivated to perform for treats in class and won't need to take an urgent bathroom break.

Leave personal belongings (including your phone!) in the car so that you can concentrate and have your hands free to hang on to the leash and use it correctly. Keep your puppy on a leash unless otherwise instructed by your trainer, and give yourself enough space so your nosy puppy can't reach other classmates. 🐾

School Days for Your Dog

A variety of schools exist to expand your dog's education. Classes run the gamut from puppy socialization to basic obedience to specialized sessions for dogs with testy temperaments. There are classes that teach dogs to become therapy canines and bring cheer to hospital patients and nursing home residents, and classes like Canine Good Citizenship that teach doggy etiquette.

The key is to look for professional dog trainers who rely on positive training techniques—not the use of physical punishment, chokers, or prong collars. I recommend that you contact the Association of Professional Dog Trainers to help you find the right trainer for you and your dog.

FIDO-SAFE FESTIVITIES

Our big family loves to celebrate holidays, anniversaries, and birthdays with all the trimmings, including decorations and plenty of special food, not to mention lots of people around. We recently adopted an energetic puppy and are wondering how to keep him from becoming a four-legged wrecking ball during our gatherings.

Your fast-growing puppy is downloading all the time: sights, sounds, smells. During holidays and when you host large gatherings, he will have to adjust to differences in the normal household routine and makeovers to the décor. From your pup's perspective, dangling decorations, especially a glittery Christmas tree, plus the aroma of cooking and baking and the excitement of extra activity can be hard to resist. Far too many emergency veterinary visits are needed because curious canines break ornaments, eat huge helpings of fatty food, or even burn their tongues by lapping at lit candles.

Since you should already have taken steps to protect your new baby in your home, one thing you can do is step up the pet-proofing. That means closing doors or installing puppy gates across openings to prevent access to a tree or other tempting decorations. Keep him out of the kitchen so he can't find chocolates, cookie dough, and other rich edibles that are unsafe for canines.

You will also need increased vigilance to prevent him from dashing out the door when guests arrive. Just in case, be sure he sports a collar with a visible identification tag, as well as a microchip. (See Let's See Some ID, page 37.)

It's often a good idea to introduce a puppy to a festive gathering on leash and only for brief periods of time. To avoid overexcitement, make sure he gets plenty of exercise and opportunities to go potty before the party starts. After a meet-and-greet session, usher him into a quiet room with a comfy spot to nap where he can chill out with a few toys. Just make sure you or someone else is attending to his needs during the festivities.

When I adopted my terrier mix, Kona, she had never lived in a home, so I went very low-key for her first Christmas with us. That meant no big tree, no breakable ornaments, and no real candles or heated potpourri. I maintained the holiday spirit by placing a small tree and battery-operated candles out of paw's reach. I strung holiday cards up high and stashed wrapped presents in a closet with the door closed until Christmas morning.

119

I also increased purposeful playtime and training with young Kona, which benefited us both. Your playful pup can be a welcome workout buddy and a healthy distraction from holiday or family stress. The true meaning of celebration is to bring joy into the lives of your family and friends and to make wonderful memories. Now your new puppy can safely be part of the celebrations and the memory making. 🐾

WHY THE DUAL DOGGY PERSONALITIES?

At dog parks and other unleashed social gatherings, my dog is friendly with other canines, but on leash, he acts like Cujo when another leashed dog approaches. What's going on here?

Alas, many otherwise well-mannered dogs transform into barking, lunging, snarling beasts in certain leashed situations. It's important to put yourself in the mind—and position—of your dog during these encounters. For starters, your dog is tethered to you with no opportunity to escape. It's the classic fight-or-flight scenario, but the flight option has been removed. Some timid dogs become master actors, pretending to be full of bravado in an attempt to keep the approaching dog at bay.

For other dogs, the leash defines a tiny territory that needs to be defended. A protective dog is warning others to stay away from the most important person on the planet—you. And dominant-minded dogs have little patience for dogs who show no canine etiquette by rushing up to them face-to-face to greet.

Second, it is vital to acknowledge that dogs are very attuned to our emotions. Without realizing it, you are probably tightening your grip on the leash or pulling your dog closer in a misguided effort to avert a barking-lunging display. Most dogs interpret that action as a signal to become even more vigilant and protective. Many will immediately shut their mouths, stare at the oncoming dog, and shift their weight to their front paws as they ready themselves for a canine confrontation.

My advice: Know your dog and set him up for success. Work on reinforcing *Walk nicely* and *Watch me* (see page 208) so that your dog has an alternative behavior. When a person with a dog approaches you, keep a firm but relaxed grip on the leash and breathe deeply in and out. Calmly and quickly position your body between your dog and the approaching dog to block them and prevent eye-to-eye stares.

Keeping your dog on your side away from the other dog, politely explain to the other person that your dog prefers his introductions off leash, and keep moving. 🐾

TO ERR IS HUMAN

I feel like a terrible dog owner. Abby, my young retriever mix, doesn't always listen to me. She is really a sweet girl, but sometimes she chases our cat, jumps up on visitors, destroys flowers in my garden, and tries to steal food from the counter. I can't help feeling frustrated and yelling at her. She cowers and leaves the room; then I feel guilty. I am tired of saying no, no, no all the time. Help!

Don't be too rough on yourself. Not even the most esteemed professional dog trainers are perfect each and every time they work with a dog. Mistakes happen. It's part of being human. One issue in your case is that Abby, like many large breeds, is taking a little longer to mature than a smaller dog would. Goldens and Labradors are generally considered "grown up" by age 2 or 3, compared with

Yorkshire terriers, who have formed their adult brains by age 1.

The key to successful training is to encourage your young dog to perform desired actions and to reward her when she nails a given command or task, rather than punishing her for bad behavior. It's also critical to provide suitable outlets for her to indulge her doggy instincts of leaping and chewing.

Take on the role of leader, not bully. There is no need to raise your voice or berate your dog. Make sure the tenor of your voice is friendly, engaging, and confident. If you are feeling frustrated, anxious, or impatient during the training lesson, Abby will pick up those emotions and the lesson will be a failure. If you can be an effective teacher who relies on positive reinforcement techniques, however, you will earn her respect, instill her with confidence, and win her love and loyalty.

Realize that puppies and teenage dogs are easily distracted. The only way to make your dog understand and comply with your training is if you have her undivided attention. For all training sessions, pick a place and a time where distractions are kept to a minimum. Start by calling your puppy by name and rewarding her for any eye contact with you.

Work on training the basics. Once you are certain your pup knows her name, you can teach her the command *Watch me* to sustain longer eye contact. Take a small food treat in your fingers and slowly bring it up to your face as you say *Watch me*. Deliver the treat to your puppy when she looks at you for at least two seconds. As she learns that she is rewarded for paying attention to you, she will be more motivated to look to you and await your next cue. (See also Training Tips, page 208.)

Be consistent, consistent, consistent. Decide which verbal and physical cues you want to use for *Sit, Lie down, Stay*, and *Come*. Then stick with them. If you use the word *Stay* in one training session and the phrase *Don't move* in the next, you create confusion. Be consistent with your commands and your dog will eventually catch on.

Opt for short training sessions. Unless you have an extremely attentive dog, training segments of 10 minutes or less will be the most effective. These mini training sessions will work better for you, too, since they fit easily into your busy schedule. It's usually possible to squeeze in a short training lesson before you head off to work or when you get home after a long day.

Think Las Vegas! Gamblers are attracted to slot machines on the chance of hitting a jackpot. The machines, by design, do not deliver a payoff with each grab of the handle. Psychologists call this *intermittent reinforcement.* Apply this theory to training your dog. Once you've taught the basics, bolster compliance by offering treats intermittently. Keep Abby guessing about when she'll be rewarded, and she'll work harder for that tasty jackpot. You can bet on it!

Take your training routine on the road. Abby may become a picture of perfect obedience inside your living room but act like a canine Dennis the Menace at the dog park. She needs to learn that she must obey you, no matter where she is and how many distractions surround her. Once you achieve success in the confines of your home, you can gradually reinforce these commands with her in other settings. You may need to start with small steps and once again build up to success. 🐾

Paying the Price

In my view, the Nothing in Life Is Free (NILIF) program offers the best payoff for most dogs and their owners. With NILIF, your dog complies with your commands and you do not need to bully or use physical force.

The idea is to bolster your leadership and cultivate your dog's respect for you by controlling all his resources. Specifically, you determine when you put his food bowl down and when you pick it up, rather than responding to his begging or letting him guard his bowl. You start and end playtime. You initiate grooming and petting sessions.

By controlling his resources, you elevate your status. I particularly like this method of training because it works with a wide range of canine personalities. Shy dogs gain confidence, distracted dogs develop focus and patience, and pushy dogs learn canine manners.

Here's how NILIF works. Start by giving your dog the cold shoulder when he demands your attention. If he paws your hand, barks at you, or brings you a toy, ignore him. Don't utter a sound or push him away. Just act like he is invisible. The message is that he cannot demand your attention anytime he desires. Eventually he will realize that you are in charge.

All members of the family must follow the new rules. Let them know that from now on, your dog must earn his paycheck (praise, treats, playtime) with proper behavior. At mealtime, ask your dog to *Sit* and *Wait* before you put the bowl down. When you want to play one of his favorite games, perhaps fetching a tennis ball, tell him to lie down before you toss the ball again. When you are done with the game, tell him *Game over*, pick up the ball, and put it out of his reach. Do this calmly and walk away.

The key to success is being consistent. Don't give in to his demands for attention, which will undoubtedly escalate in the beginning of this new routine. Every time you want to toss your dog a small treat, have him do something—sit or do a trick—before you hand it over. Make sure he knows that you always exit and enter doors before he does.

NILIF establishes a clear ranking in the household, with you in the number one spot. It is done without meanness but rather as a simple fact of life. In time, your dog will come to view you as the Provider of All Things Wonderful, and you will be amazed how much he will come to appreciate this clarity and be more responsive to your cues.

HEY! COME BACK HERE!

I thought teaching my dog to come to me would be a snap. Boy, was I wrong! Higgins is a 6-month-old mixed breed with a mind of his own. I find myself yelling at him over and over to come back to me and becoming so frustrated that I scold him when he finally does. It's getting worse. When I take him to the local dog park, I sometimes have to chase him to put the leash on him when it is time to go. How can I get Higgins to come when I call him?

You must train your dog to come when you call. There are three basic commands that are doggone vital: *Come, Sit*, and *Stay*. These commands can be lifesavers. An obedient dog responds to *Come* and turns toward you rather than chasing a cat into a busy street. Unlike a trained dog who ignores his owner's calls in favor of an alluring odor, it sounds as though Higgins has never learned to come in the first place.

When he is running around loose, he probably has no idea what you want and no real interest in finding out. Higgins is a canine teenager and has entered the stage in life when he feels the need to test and challenge authority. He needs to clearly know who's in charge, and that should be you.

When you overuse any command without getting results, it loses value. Repeating a cue that your dog ignores just teaches him that he doesn't have to do anything. Some dogs will wait until their owners say *Come* a dozen times before they turn their heads. Smart dogs quickly learn that *Come* means "keep running around sniffing until my owner grabs me."

Another easy misstep is to overspeak when you want Higgins to come. You must pick a cue and use it consistently. If you call out, "Hey, Higgins, I want you to come here right now, I'm not joking, Higgins, I really mean it, I want you to come now," Higgins, in true doggy fashion, is most likely to translate all that chatter into "Higgins, blah, blah, blah, blah" and will never respond because your cue got lost in translation.

There are many ways to teach Higgins to come when you call (see Training Tips, page 208), but here is one creative way to grab his attention. If he loves to shred squeaky toys, keep a squeaker from one of those ruined toys. Call him once, then press the squeaker as you slowly walk away from him. I guarantee his attention will shift to you. When he comes, praise and treat.

In addition, here are three other game plans to try. Conduct your initial training sessions in a confined area like

125

you call out *Higgins, come!* in an upbeat, happy voice. As soon as he finds you, give him a treat, say *Yes!*, and repeat the game in a different room. This makes finding you lots of fun for Higgins and builds a positive connection to the command.

Game Plan C: Play tag. Lightly tap Higgins on the back and say, *Tag, you're it!* Then race away. When Higgins pursues you and reaches you, praise him and give a treat. If he doesn't follow you, stop a few feet away, keep your back to him, and bend down. Pretend you are looking at the world's most fascinating blade of grass or carpet fiber. Curiosity will get the best of Higgins, and he will come up to investigate what is so darn riveting. Again, praise and treat. The goal is to always have your dog chase after you, not you chasing after your dog.

Practice all three of these games in your home and in confined areas without a lot of distractions. Please do not let Higgins run loose in open spaces near streets where he could get hit by a car. Always end these mini sessions on a good note. When he comes back quickly, praise and treat and move on.

Once Higgins consistently heeds your calls to him, then test his responsiveness in an enclosed backyard or dog park with only one or two other dogs around. Gradually, build up his recall until Higgins responds even in high canine traffic, such as a dog park on a Saturday morning. 🐾

your backyard or a hallway or another place without a lot of distractions or possibilities for escape. You want him to focus on you.

Game Plan A: Change your attitude. It is easy to be feel peeved when your dog dashes around ignoring you. But because of your harsh tones, Higgins associates the word *Come* with repri-mands. Why should he return only to be scolded? Solution: Switch to a new word, like *Here* or *Now* or even *Bye*.

I used the latter with my dog Jazz when he stopped heeding the *Come* cue. I would simply say *Bye*, turn my back on him, and walk in the opposite direction. He was back in a flash by my side. I then praised him. Even when Higgins takes his sweet time at returning, never yell at him for coming back.

Game Plan B: Make it child's play by modifying the hide-and-seek game. In your house, have a family member or friend keep Higgins on a leash as you scurry into another room out of his view. Your helper then unleashes Higgins as

HEY, HEY, WHY DON'T YOU STAY?

My neighbor Paul has a very obedient Rottweiler named Gus. If Paul tells Gus to *Stay*, that dog will sit or lie down and not move until Paul tells him it is okay. He will wait quietly while Paul goes into the corner store to pick up milk or has a cup of coffee in a café. My big, friendly mutt, Moose, won't stay put for a second. I have a little bit of canine envy. How can I get Moose to behave as well as Gus?

Sometimes we need our dogs to remain in one place until we say they can move. Teaching your dog to stay is handy when you want him not to bolt out of your house or car when you open the door or when the family cat enters the room and you don't want your dog to give chase. You are teaching Moose that if he stays in one spot until you say otherwise, he will be safe. He learns that even if you disappear from view into a store, you will return (with praise for his good behavior, of course!).

You can teach Moose to stay on cue, but don't expect overnight success. He should know *Sit* and *Down* before beginning to work on this more complicated behavior. As you teach Moose to stay, keep the training sessions short and fun and always end on a good note. If Moose seems to struggle a bit, don't move forward until he consistently succeeds in the earlier steps.

Mastering the *Stay* command involves duration, distance, and distractions. At first, only expect Moose to stay for a moment while you stand next to him and there is nothing else going on around you. Put him on a long leash at first, so you can control him if he tries to move. Your goal is to gradually expand the amount of time Moose complies and the amount of space between the two of

Breed Byte

During the Middle Ages in Germany, butchers traveling to buy livestock would fasten their moneybags around the muscular necks of their Rottweilers to dissuade would-be thieves.

127

you. The final element involves Moose staying put despite distractions such as other dogs or squirrels.

When training a dog, you need eye contact and undivided attention from him. First teach Moose the *Watch me* cue. Teach this by saying his name and telling him *Watch me* as you take a small food treat and move it toward the side of your eye. The goal is to get him to watch the treat move. When he does, hand over the treat.

Next, put him in a *Down* or *Sit* position. Wait a second or two before you say *Stay!* as you use your hand in a motion like a traffic cop signaling halt to oncoming cars, and then reward with a treat. Purposely delay the reward to teach your dog that you are requesting him to stay put.

With each successful stay, gradually extend the time you reward a treat from 2 to 5 to 10 seconds and on up to a minute. If Moose should get up and move before the designated time, do not give a treat. Do not punish him, either—just return him to his original position and tell him to *Stay* again.

When you are ready to have Moose move, give him a specific release word and hand signal. I use the word *Okay* with a sweeping motion of my open-palmed hand. You could say *We're done* or *Release*. Pick a term you prefer and will remember.

When Moose is solid for a minute, add the distance element by putting Moose in a stay and moving about five feet away while he is still on a leash. Reward him for staying until you return to him. Slowly build on his success by dropping the leash and expanding the distance between you. As he learns, add to the difficulty by walking behind him and moving around him. Again, if he breaks from his stay, just return him to position and start again.

The final step is to introduce distractions. After all, your dog does not live in a bubble that you'll always be able to control. Things happen—a squirrel will suddenly appear on the sidewalk, or a skateboard will whiz by—and Moose may want to give chase. That's where the *Stay* command keeps him by your side. Start with mild distractions, such as having someone clap their hands as a noise distraction.

Take your training outside and have a friend walk by as you tell Moose to *Stay*. Ask your neighbor Paul to help for a few training sessions by walking Gus past while Moose shows how much he's learned. Go slowly and encourage Moose. Most of all, be patient. Deliver treats and praise only when your dog ignores the increasingly tempting distractions and stays put. (See also Training Tips, page 208.) 🐾

IGNORING TEMPTATION

My elderly mom lives with us and needs to take medication for her heart and for high blood pressure. I worry that she may accidentally spill a pill on the floor and Pebbles, my pug, will think it is food and eat it and get sick. Pebbles constantly has her nose to the ground to sniff out anything edible. Is there any way I can teach her to keep her from eating something she shouldn't?

You are right to be concerned about Pebbles accidentally mistaking a pill for a food find. With her small size, she could become very sick and possibly even die from swallowing human medication. However, it is canine nature to explore using the nose and the mouth. After all, our thumbless dogs can't pick up a tempting object in their paws and scrutinize it. They are designed to sniff and sample.

It is far better to be safe and prepared by teaching your dog the cues *Leave it* and *Drop it*. These behaviors work in partnership, so think of them as the Dynamic Duo for Dog Safety. They are effective whenever you need your dog to ignore something within reach or to release something already in her mouth, such as the TV remote or a bottle of pills.

Poison Hotline

If you ever suspect that your dog has swallowed human medication or any toxic substance, call the ASPCA Animal Poison Control Center Hotline toll-free at 888-426-4435. Please note there is a consultation fee that can be applied to your credit card, but it is worth the price if you save your pet's life.

Put the hotline number and the contact information of your own veterinarian and the nearest emergency veterinary clinic in your list of contacts on your phone for quick reference.

To begin, put Pebbles on a leash and practice in a quiet room in your house to avoid other distractions. Teach her to *Leave it* first. Your mission is to stop her before she can put the object in her mouth. Put a treat in your hand and make a fist. Without her knowing, hide a second treat nearby. Let Pebbles smell your hand. She will probably lick your hand, paw at it, and try to get you to surrender the treat to her.

Practice some patience. Wait for her to give up and stop pawing at your closed hand for a few seconds. Then, praise her and hand over the hidden treat. Repeat this until Pebbles catches on that by honoring your *Leave it* request, she gets the goodies.

You can then up the ante. Put Pebbles on a leash and bring out two types of treats: so-so and delicious. Drop a piece or two of the so-so treat on the ground in front of Pebbles and tell her to *Leave it*. Restrain her with the leash if necessary. Once she ignores the temptation, hand over a few of the better treats to her and praise her. Practice this often on your walks to reinforce the desired behavior in different situations.

Teach the *Drop it* command next. Start by enticing Pebbles with one of her B-list toys. Let her put the toy in her mouth and play with it for a minute or so and then show her one of her all-time favorite toys. When you get her attention, show her a yummy treat. As soon as she opens her mouth, say *Drop it* and hand over the treat. You are pairing the phrase *Drop it* with the behavior—releasing the toy from her mouth.

Praise her when she lets go of the first toy and approaches you to take the second toy. Vary the objects (always getting her to trade up to a more desirable object) to expand her understanding of the *Drop it* request.

A final pointer: Resist shouting *Drop it* in an urgent tone while you chase after your dog. If you are overly annoyed or emotional, your dog will either swallow the goody fast or run with it, thinking it has value. The best strategy is to speak calmly (even though you may be quite upset) and reward with a high-value treat. 🐾

WHO'S THE BOSS?

At first, we thought it was cute when our Scottish terrier puppy growled playfully whenever we tried to stop her from stealing a sock or tried to take a toy away from her. But Mimi is now nearly a year old and her growls don't seem so harmless. She hasn't bitten anyone, but she definitely sounds like she means business. What can we do to stop this behavior from escalating?

It may seem amusing when a puppy commandeers a sock or keeps you at bay when you try to take a toy from her, but this is a very bad habit to let her develop. Left undisciplined, many dogs will begin to view themselves as the leader of the household and will progress from growling to snapping at, or even biting, people who challenge them.

This type of aggression may surface between 12 and 24 months of age as a dog gains physical and social maturity. Any aggression directed at owners can make the owners frustrated and fearful and the dog uneasy and anxious, setting up a vicious circle of behavior. Untreated, this canine bullying will only intensify. This is a particularly important time for you to be firm, fair, and consistent. Be aware that showering such a dog with affection, giving her unearned treats, and allowing her free rein in the house may reinforce this behavior, because the dog feels that her place as top dog is being rewarded.

It's important that you become a VIP (Very Influential Person) in Mimi's view while she is demoted to PHD (Pretty Humble Pup). Instead of trying to match growl for growl, you need to become the household's benevolent leader whom your dog looks up to, the person who has more influence over your dog than anything else in the world.

To begin with, if Mimi shows any sign of aggression, give her the cold shoulder by calmly putting her in a bathroom. Close the door and give her a brief

time-out (less than five minutes). When you open the door, ignore her for about 30 seconds. Banishment and withdrawal of attention are the most potent forms of correction because they remove a dog's ability to control a situation. Then, return her to the scene and try again for success.

There are several ways to promote yourself in Mimi's eyes. Start by enforcing good manners. She needs to sit for her meals and wait while you put her bowl down. You can hand-feed her to help her learn that hands are for offering treats rather than grabbing toys. Instead of taking items away from her, teach her *Drop it* (see Ignoring Temptation, page 129). Train her to find her spot (see Find Your Spot, Spot!, below) when company arrives.

The key is consistency, so everyone in the household needs to follow the new rules. By becoming a better leader who is gentle but firm, you will have better control of the situation, and Mimi will likely stop growling and will display friendlier behavior. If her behavior does not improve, however, I favor being proactive and seeking help from an animal behaviorist before growls turn into lunges or biting attacks. 🐾

FIND YOUR SPOT, SPOT!

Whenever I get ready to leave the house or when I first come in the front door, my dog, Katie, is always underfoot. She wiggles her whole body, wags her tail a mile a minute, tries to jump on me, and gives me kisses. More than once, I've spilled a bag of groceries because I've tripped over her or tried to reach down to pet her in an attempt to quiet her down. I love Katie, but what can I do so that I can come and go without this over-the-top demonstration of affection?

Now you know how a rock star or other celebrity feels when surrounded by adoring but obnoxious fans. Katie is doing all she can to deliver canine love your way, even at the sacrifice of some groceries. Her slightly pushy behavior has worked so far in getting what she wants, which is your attention. Here is one way you can redirect Katie's enthusiasm to allow you to walk in and out without having to play dodge dog. (See Clingy Canine, page 158, and Look Out for Launching Lab!, page 65, for other strategies.)

Situate a dog bed somewhere near your door where your dog can see you but not be in the way. Whenever you have five minutes and are in a patient mood, call Katie. Have her sit and stay somewhere else in the room while you toss a treat on the doggy bed. Make her stay until you excitedly call out *Find your spot* as you point to the treat on the bed. Encourage Katie as she dashes to the bed to grab the treat. Praise her and have her stay on the bed for a few seconds.

Repeat this scenario several times. With each success, extend the time that she stays on her bed. Now you're ready to toss a treat and ask her to find her spot and stay there as you head out the door. Give her premium treats when she hits her mark even with the excitement of having you enter the house. (See also Training Tips, page 208.)

Find your spot works wonders when you need to greet someone at your door, want your dog to wait quietly as you leave the house, or anytime you need her not to be underfoot. It's also a good technique for a socially anxious dog who barks at guests.

In my house, *Find your spot!* generates a lot of anticipation and excitement because Kona never knows which of her favorite treats she will get until she lands on the doggy bed in the family room. Sometimes, I put peanut butter in a hollow synthetic bone. Other times, I give her a dental chew or a handful of dried turkey treats. We both know the routine. I grab the treats and my car keys as Kona watches. Then I call out in a happy tone, *Find your spot!* That's her cue to race to her bed with a triumphant leap to happily await her surprise goodies. I hand over the treats, tell her in a calm voice that I'll be back, and walk out the door.

I use this command at bedtime, too, to get Kona to tuck herself in her bed so I can brush my teeth and wash my face without tripping over her. 🐾

SEEKING LOVE ON A LEASH

Callie, my happy Brittany spaniel, yanks and pulls constantly on the leash when I take her for a walk. If she wants to smell something a few feet ahead, she takes off with no regard for my shoulder or wrist. She charges back and forth in front of me or drags behind to check out different smells. Walking her is not fun. It is trying and tiring. I scold her, but she just ignores me and keeps on pulling. What can I do so that she walks politely on a leash?

Sounds like walking Callie is literally a drag, but you have plenty of company. There are legions of leash-yanking dogs all over the globe. Right now, Callie doesn't understand that you want her to behave a certain way on your walks. She is just excited to be outside sniffing around. It can be challenging to rein in a dog on a "gotta sniff here, there, and everywhere" canine quest. Success hinges on improving her focus on you, using the right equipment, and developing your "benevolent boss" status, plus a lot of patience.

What doesn't work is yanking back. When a dog feels pressure on her throat, she responds by leaning into that pressure to get away from it. Yanking on the leash doesn't teach her to stop pulling and can injure her neck and trachea. In a continuous cycle, you keep losing this leash tug-of-war, which reinforces her determination to yank even more.

You need to start by increasing your own "curb appeal" so that Callie pays attention to you rather than to that squirrel scampering up the oak tree, that stray soccer ball kicked in your path, or that beckoning smell left on your route by the cute Westie up the street. Before you head out the door, prepare a bag of treats cut into tiny pieces. Teach Callie the *Watch me* command, so she will look your way when you speak those magic words. Each time Callie heeds your cue, immediately dole out a small treat.

Practice inside the house for a few days first and then on the sidewalk in front of your house. Then walk a bit and call *Watch me* again. Treat her sporadically, so Callie never knows when a reward will occur. Dogs will perform more consistently if they aren't rewarded every single time they respond. (See also Training Tips, page 208.)

You also need the right tools. Avoid choke or prong collars. Some dogs react to these by becoming testy and aggressive, and if used improperly, these collars can cause injury. Instead, opt for a nylon head halter (such as a Gentle

Leader or Halti), which fits behind your dog's ears with a loop over the nose. The leash is attached to a metal ring below your dog's chin. It comes with directions, but if you're not sure how to properly fit one on your dog, seek the help of a dog trainer or your veterinarian.

The halter works by applying pressure to the dog's nose instead of her throat. Because the nose is more sensitive than the neck, she will back away from the pressure rather than leaning into it. You can also use a no-pull harness that puts pressure on the dog's chest, with the leash attached to a D-ring on the dog's back. Some harnesses have the ring on the dog's chest.

Remember that the halter and other similar types of equipment should be viewed as training aids to help you train your dog. It is not the equipment itself but how it is used that makes it effective or dangerous.

Let me emphasize that a head halter is not a muzzle. It doesn't prevent your dog from being able to breathe, pant, drink, chew, or pick up toys or treats. It does control her head movement without causing pain and with a minimum of effort, which will save your shoulder muscles. It also doesn't need to be a lifelong accessory. Once your dog learns the habit of walking politely, you can gradually wean her off the head halter if you like.

Introduce the new gear inside the house at first. Let Callie sniff and inspect it. Put it on her and distract her with treats if she tries to rub it off (something many dogs will attempt). Keep the mood light and playful, and do not reprimand her for trying to remove it. Then take her out for a short walk with the goal of getting her to associate the head halter with two fun doggy pleasures: a walk and treats.

As a dog's head goes, so goes the direction of her body. A slight tug on the leash will automatically move Callie's head back to look at you. No longer focused on moving forward, she should

135

stop and look to you to see what's next. Let a few seconds pass, and then resume the walk or abruptly change directions or pace. Keep her guessing. Reward her for keeping her attention on you.

If *Watch me* and the halter aren't working as well as you'd like, act like a tree. Trees don't move. If Callie starts to yank, stop and remain still. Do not move forward again until the leash is slack. Or take a couple of quick steps backward until she pays attention. Once she is focused on you, resume walking and dole out treats only when the leash is slack, not tight.

When Callie is walking easily, point out her good behavior by using the proper word. Some people say *Heel*, but I think *Walk nicely* sounds more civilized. Praise Callie and reward her for stretches of walking nicely.

Training a dog to stop tugging on her leash takes time and patience, but the payoff is worth it. The two of you can enjoy your walks together, and your role as leader will become more firmly established, which will only benefit your whole relationship. 🐾

Taking Baby Steps

Parents of babies and toddlers often struggle to manage walks around the neighborhood with both a dog and a stroller. Large or small, a dog who runs in front of the wheels or lags behind can spell disaster. (See Seeking Love on a Leash, page 134, for tips on using a head halter, which is usually very effective.)

Other tips include using a special leash that clips around your waist to keep your hands free, although these are best suited for smaller dogs. If your dog is a lively Lab or a big bullmastiff, you might opt for the head halter instead. Some active parents put their older babies in backpack carriers designed for infants. This will allow you to keep both hands free and have better control of the leash.

Another idea is to enlist a friend or neighbor to walk with you—someone who is willing to take over either the stroller or the leash so that you can stroll more safely.

PIDDLY PUDDLES

My best friend has three young adult miniature pinschers who don't seem to understand that their bathroom is outside. Her house has wall-to-wall carpeting, and when I visit, I am taken aback by the smell of urine. The dogs may be small, but the smell is strong. My friend always apologizes and dismisses the severity of the problem by saying the puddles are small and cleanup is easy and quick.

I've had dogs all my life and currently have a large poodle who lets me know when she must go outside. She never makes messes in my house. Any advice on how to help my friend?

If I were to identify the primary negative trait of miniature pinschers, difficulty in house-training would top the list, though this trait applies to many toy breeds. Part of the problem is that tiny dogs physically can't hold their bladders for as long as bigger dogs, but often, the issue is that the owners don't insist on house-training as rigorously as they would with a large dog.

Some people with small breeds such as Yorkshire terriers, pugs, min pins, and dachshunds worry about putting their precious pets out in cold or wet weather or can dismiss their messes as minor lapses and overlook them. But small piddles and poops still add up to a big problem that needs to be corrected.

Dogs do not naturally house-train themselves—they all need help to learn proper bathroom habits. In your friend's case, she has not properly house-trained her min pin trio, and her house is paying the consequences. It is time for you to level with her about the odor in her home. Other guests to her house may not say anything to her but will be less apt to make return visits.

Offer to work with your friend and her dogs. Take her trio to the veterinary clinic to make sure they do not have any medical condition that may be causing them to have weak bladders. Most likely, however, they urinate indoors because they don't know the difference or they are each marking their own territory within the house with their signature scent. Male and female dogs will both display marking behavior, especially if they have not been neutered or spayed. Studies show a dramatic drop in this unwanted behavior following sterilization surgery.

Your friend must start from the beginning and completely retrain her dogs if she wants to solve this problem. Ask if she is amenable to crate training her trio or confining them in one room (like a kitchen or other room with an uncarpeted floor) when she can't be home to supervise them. Establish a routine in which the dogs are ushered outside as soon they wake up in the morning, after every meal, after play-time, and right before bed.

Encourage your friend to praise each dog each time they do their business outside. If she catches a dog in the act inside, she should clap her hands loudly to startle and distract him long enough to grab him and take him outside. Once he does go to the bathroom outside, she can heap on the praise and give a treat.

Accidents will happen during the training process, but it is important not to become angry or frustrated. When you vent those emotions, training stops, and your dogs just become fearful or confused. It is futile, and foolish, to pun-ish dogs when they urinate or defecate in the house. All they will learn is to do their business secretly or when their owner is not around.

Another step your friend must take is to thoroughly clean all her carpeting and furniture with an enzyme-based product that actually eliminates odor by destroying the protein molecules in urine and feces rather than covering it up with another smell. There are many pet cleanup products on the market that work this way. Do not use any products with ammonia, because it smells enough like urine to actually attract dogs back to the scene of their crime.

When her dogs are thoroughly trained to go outdoors only and not to have accidents in the house, it sounds as though she will need to replace a great deal of carpeting and padding. When she shops for new flooring, tell her to consider pet-friendly types like tile or laminate! 🐾

QUIT BEGGING, COLD TURKEY

My 7-year-old cocker spaniels, Billy and Bessie, are champions at begging for food. Each one takes a position on either side of me at dinner. Every time I put a forkful in my mouth, I can feel two sets of brown eyes boring into me. They really work on me, and I end up succumbing to their begging and giving them a little bit of food from my plate.

The problem is getting worse. They are now targeting my dinner guests, some of whom do not take kindly to dogs watching them eat. Is it too late to stop this behavior?

Who can resist those soulful eyes? That slight drool and subtle whimper for a piece of meatloaf or a spoonful of gravy? Billy and Bessie have learned that when people gather around the dining room table, goodies seem to fall from the sky. With such rewards, of course their begging behavior is increasing.

Unfortunately, some charming beggars transform into thugs who aggressively try to take food from you. Others gain too much weight from nibbling on high-fat people food and become ideal candidates for diabetes, heart problems, arthritis, and other health problems. A little bit of leftover chicken or steak won't hurt, but it's important to limit their intake.

My father used to love pulling up to the drive-through window and ordering cheeseburgers for himself and his dog, Keesha. He stopped when Keesha became very ill with pancreatitis, a potentially fatal disease. My dad never conquered his own fast-food cravings, but he did make smarter choices for Keesha after that. Instead of a burger, she enjoyed a healthy dog treat from the glove compartment. She slimmed down and became healthier as a result.

As for your chowhound duo, it is never too late to break the begging habit. When you start the retraining regime, it may be easiest to usher them into another room when you have company, so you and your guests can dine in peace. Turn on a radio or other distraction and give them treat balls with holes that they must nose around to make kibble and other goodies fall out. This makes them work for their treats and keeps them occupied while you enjoy your dinner.

When it's just the family, start a new regime immediately by not giving food from your plate to Billy and Bessie. They need to learn that dogs should be neither seen nor heard at the table. Completely ignore their pleas for food (after all, you know they are not starving). Expect their begging behavior to become worse before it improves, because they will think that if it worked before, more of the same will work again.

For this to work, everyone at the table needs to ignore both dogs completely. Don't even tell them "no begging!" If Billy and Bessie persist, then have them do a *Down*, *Stay*, or *Go to your spot* while the family is eating. This gives them something to do while you finish your meal.

You cannot succeed without enlisting the aid of your friends and family members. Explain that you do not wish to have Billy and Bessie fed from the table. Let them know that you're doing this out of concern for the health of your dogs and the comfort of your guests. If everyone at the table ignores the dogs (no eye contact, no talking, no petting—nothing!), they will eventually learn that begging no longer yields a reward and that the proper place for treats is in their bowls after the people leave the table. 🐾

Breed Byte

The cocker spaniel is the smallest member of the sporting-dog family.

PUT THE BRAKES ON CHASING

I need help controlling my gotta-chase terrier mix. No critter is spared. Boomer darts after squirrels and ducks during our walks and turns our home into a raceway by chasing our cat. How can I find the stop button on my dog?

Ah, the art of the chase! Many dogs automatically take off after anything that runs. There is a genetic component to chasing, which explains why terriers dash madly after fast-moving squirrels, fleeing felines, and even inanimate objects such as moving skateboards.

Since cats and squirrels are Boomer's preferred prey, let's look at what's happening with him. Some dogs chase small animals for fun; others chase to kill. From both instinct and practice, many dogs know how to grab and shake a small animal all in one motion and break its spine. Distinguishing a playful chase from pure predatory instinct is not easy, and you definitely don't want to find out the hard way if Boomer is out for a romp or in for the kill. You need to stop his chasing behavior before he hurts a neighbor's pet or chases a squirrel out in front of a moving car.

Identify as many specifics as possible when Boomer bursts into chase mode. Pay attention to the time of day, the location, the object being chased, and his specific actions. The more details, the better you will be able to predict his reactions and intercede to curb the chase desire. By doing this doggy detective work, you can identify a predictable pattern that will help you to come up with an effective treatment plan.

One strategy is to teach Boomer the command *Watch me* (see page 208). Work on this behavior inside without distractions before trying it outside. Don't feed Boomer before a training session. You want him a little hungry so he will pay more attention to you. Have plenty of treats with you and keep him on a 4-foot-long leash while he learns to pay attention to you.

Each time you spot a squirrel or bird, reorient him by telling him *Watch me*. Then have him sit politely to earn a treat while he ignores the temptation. The goal is for him to learn a new association. As he discovers that he gets a prized treat whenever he sees a squirrel, he will look to you instead of speeding after it.

As for your cat, it is never too late to work on your dog's cat-greeting skills. Be sure to provide your cat with dog-free zones and stress-free escape routes. Until Boomer consistently stops chasing your cat, separate them when you are not around to supervise.

Teach Boomer these obedience commands: *Down* and *Stay*. (See Training Tips, page 208.) Set him up for success by attaching a long leash or clothesline to his collar to control his movement inside your home, especially when your cat enters the room.

Keep a bag of treats handy. When your dog eyes your cat, redirect his attention by showing him a treat. Calmly instruct him to *Sit* or *Down* or *Stay*. Do not yell, because you will only heighten his excitement and your cat's fearfulness. If your dog ignores your command and starts to chase your cat, step on the leash to stop him.

You'll need to be patient, as the chase drive is very strong in terriers, and holding a *Stay* is challenging. Changing Boomer's behavior may take a lot of time and repeated commands. In addition to teaching Boomer better self-control, work on improving his recall so that he can chase after an acceptable object such as a tennis ball or dog toy. When he heeds your call to *Come*, reward him by flinging the acceptable toy in different directions and encourage him to chase after it. 🐾

Canine Jocks Rule!

Do you share your home with a four-legged jock? Once you've laid down a foundation of basic obedience training, there are lots of organized sports activities for you and your dog to enjoy together. Here are a few to think about.

Agility. This sport appeals to dogs who love to conquer obstacle courses. Whether for fun or for competition, agility challenges dogs to wiggle through weave poles, jump through tires, climb up and down ramps, and dash through tunnels. This sport is all about posting clean runs and quick times.

Learn more about the various groups sponsoring agility events by visiting the United States Dog Agility Association (USDAA), open to dogs of all sizes and breeds. Another resource is the North American Dog Agility Council. Purebreds registered with the American Kennel Club can compete in AKC agility.

Disc dogs. This sport caters to dogs of all breeds and mixes who love to chase, leap, and snag plastic discs hurled into the air by their owners. Points are based on the distance and difficulty of the catch. For more details, visit the websites of Skyhoundz, the Ashley Whippet Invitational, the United States Disc Dog Nationals, or the UFO World Cup Series (see Useful Websites, page 214).

Flyball. Does your dog love to play tag and catch balls? Flyball may be his sport. Flyball is a relay race involving four-dog teams. Each dog zips down a lane, leaping over hurdles, to catch a launched tennis ball and race back to his starting point. The fastest team wins. To learn more, contact the North American Flyball Association.

Herding. Some dogs have built-in abilities to shepherd sheep, cattle, and other animals from Point A to Point B without bullying or harming the livestock. Learn more by visiting the American Herding Breed Association's website.

Lure coursing. For dogs with a strong chase drive, this sport uses an artificial lure connected to a long line strung around a series of pulleys. The lure zigzags around a course with points awarded based on a dog's speed and ability to follow it. More information is available at the American Sighthound Field Association or the American Kennel Club.

Scent work. What dog doesn't like to use his nose to sniff out clues? In this sport, dogs search for a wide range of scents and substances hidden in a specified search area. This is definitely a sport that requires dog-people teamwork. Learn more at the National Association of Canine Scent Work or from the American Kennel Club.

Dock diving. This fun sport is literally making a big splash. The rules are simple: You toss your dog's favorite toy in a pool while he is 40 feet back on a dock in a sit. He sprints when you tell him to go, and you time the throw with the hope he catches his toy as he splashes into the pool. The winner is the dog who achieves the longest jump. Learn more at the website for North America Diving Dogs.

Canine musical freestyle. Love to dance with your dog? This sport spotlights human and dog partners doing choreographed moves to music. To learn more, check out the Canine Freestyle Federation or the World Canine Freestyle Organization.

ACHIEVING HEALTH
and Harmony at Home and Away

Your home should be your castle, not a palace of canine chaos. Who wants to enter the front door and be tackled by a blur of fur? Or cancel a date because your dog growls at your boyfriend? Or lose a good night's sleep because your poodle hogs the pillow? Yet when it comes to who spends the most time actually in our homes, dogs win paws down.

No longer relegated to the backyard, most pet dogs are regarded as favored companions, preferred roommates, and valued members of the family. Adding dogs to the mix of spouses, children, housemates, and other pets can make it a challenge to achieve harmony in your home.

Each person and each species must understand and honor the house rules to prevent snarling and snapping.

Fortunately, dogs crave consistency and they want to know where they rank in the household hierarchy. They depend on us to teach them proper canine etiquette around babies, children, and houseguests. They look to us to learn if the sofa can be a comfy sanctuary or if it is off-limits. Our dogs can't contribute to paying the mortgage, but their presence in our lives can truly be a priceless pleasure—if they know their place in the pack.

And dogs are often the go-to companion for on-the-road adventures. More hotels are putting out the welcome mat for well-mannered pets, as are outdoor patios at restaurants. I travel a lot with my dogs, especially Pet Safety Dog Kona, who joins me at conferences and pet events. She digs road trips, and so might your four-legged friend.

COUCH POTATO PUP

I don't go to the gym as often as I used to, and I seem to spend more time binge-watching shows on Netflix. Unfortunately, my dog is following my lazy ways. He doesn't get excited when I bring out his leash and harness for a long walk and isn't as eager to sprint after balls I toss for him in the backyard. He is about 8 and has an all-okay checkup from my veterinarian. What can I do to add a little pep to his steps—and mine?

It is easy to become couch-bound, especially with so many choices of shows to watch and the convenience of having great meals delivered to your door. Energy zappers can strike any dog, no matter the age, breed, or size. But as you know, you and your dog will both benefit from getting up and moving.

Experts in pet nutrition and fitness concur that a healthy weight, a sound digestive system, and a vital immune system are the key factors in your dog staying energetic and engaged. Fortunately, healthy energy boosters for dogs—and their people—come in many forms.

Here are some of my favorites for your consideration.

Dish up clean H₂O. Never underestimate the power of hydration. Dogs need access to plenty of clean water to maintain healthy body temperatures, sport hydrated muscles and joints, produce healthy poops, and flush out bacteria that may trigger urinary tract infections. (I also add a pet-safe dental preventive in all of my pets' water bowls every day to fend off tartar buildup.)

Treat your dog to sunlight. Studies show that just like people, dogs can suffer from seasonal affective disorder if they do not receive adequate exposure to sunlight. This can cause them to become depressed, act lethargic, and lose their appetites.

Be extra vigilant during winter months when days are shorter and during periods of steady rain by timing walks before the sun goes down and during breaks in rain showers. Expose your dog to natural vitamin D by locating his bed by a sunny window or under a skylight. Talk to your veterinarian about the possible benefits of purchasing an artificial sunlight lamp to use indoors for your dog.

Banish boredom eating. Mealtime is of key importance to your dog, and you can use that fact to reinforce obedience cues and maybe learn a new trick or two. Like humans, dogs can succumb to boredom eating. Skip the food bowl once or twice a week and get your dog to work his brain by finding food hidden in a puzzle toy or take him on a "food safari" to hunt for food hidden somewhere else in the house.

Heap on the blues, greens, and oranges. Boost your dog's immune system and pump up his digestion by topping his meals with blueberries (loaded with antioxidants), steamed green beans or kale (packed with vitamins A, C, and E), or canned puréed pumpkin (full of fiber and carotenoids; just make sure you're not giving him sugar-laden pumpkin pie filling).

Jazz up your daily walks. Instead of your usual circuit around the block, occasionally treat your dog to unstructured walks, allowing him to sniff where he wants for as long as he wants. Veterinary behaviorists says that these "sniff walks" may help boost a dog's mood and energy level.

Ignore the weather! When it's too cold or rainy to go outside, temporarily convert your living room or other space into a canine gym. Set up a mini obstacle course with paper plates or books and weave through them with your dog on a short leash, or prop a broom on a couple of books and encourage your dog to hop over it. Play chase or fetch in the hallway or indulge in a friendly tug-of-war with a sturdy toy—anything to get you both off the couch! 🐾

PAWS DE DEUX

Laddie is a high-energy border collie mix we adopted as a puppy about a year ago. We love him, but he constantly wants to play with us and he never seems to tire. If we ignore him, he grabs a toy and shoves it in front of our faces or drops it in our laps so we'll toss it for him to retrieve. A couple of times a week, we take him to the local dog park, where he zooms around and seems to enjoy himself.

We're thinking about getting a second dog in hopes of giving Laddie a playmate to romp with so that he doesn't demand so much of our attention. We've visited a few local animal shelters, but we want to know what we should look for in a second dog and how to properly introduce a new dog to our home.

Border collies are notoriously energetic and active, so it's not surprising that Laddie is always on the go. You are right to provide him with suitable outlets such as visits to a dog park, but once or twice a week won't cut it, especially for a dog this young and spirited. He needs brisk walks, preferably twice a day, that last at least 20 minutes.

The fact that Laddie enjoys dog parks is a good sign that he likes canine company. Use your dog park outings to scope out what type of dogs he seems to enjoy the most. Pay attention to the dog's personality more than the breed. Laddie might like a dog equal to his playful manner, or he might prefer a quieter, calmer pal.

Once you have narrowed down a list of three or four potential candidates at your local shelter, you're ready to test compatibility. Arrange a time at the shelter to bring Laddie to meet each dog one at a time. Many shelters provide meet-and-greet areas for just this purpose. Introductions should be conducted on neutral turf, not at your home, to reduce the likelihood of Laddie seeing the other dog as a territorial intruder.

Set yourself and Laddie up for success by bringing a dog-savvy friend or family member to assist you. You should each have a pocketful of tasty treats. Your goal is to make this an upbeat, positive event for both dogs. Take Laddie on his leash as your friend keeps the other dog on a leash. Speak in a happy voice and let the two dogs briefly do the "canine handshake" (sniffing each other's butts). Dogs are more likely to become aggressive if they are face-to-face, so avoid a head-on confrontation. After 10 seconds or so, separate the two dogs. Give them each a treat.

If the dogs behave, you're ready for the second step: taking them for a short walk. Position the dogs on the outside with you and your friend in the middle; don't let them wander too far in front of you at first. Continue talking to them in a positive voice. Stop occasionally, ask them to *Sit*, and give them treats. Then continue walking. Periodically, let them approach each other for an updated sniff. If they seem relaxed, you can give them some more room on the leashes, but be careful of tangles if they start to play.

After a successful walk, let them loose together in an enclosed space, if one is available. Dogs often act very differently when leashed—many are better at making friends off leash.

During this introduction, pay close attention to each dog's posture. Good signs include play bowing, open mouths with relaxed facial muscles, and one acting submissive to the other (by lying down and exposing his belly for the other to sniff). Be wary if either dog bares his teeth, emits deep growls, stares directly, or assumes a stiff-legged stance. If this happens, see if you can defuse the tension by calling the dog over to you, asking him to *Sit*, and giving a treat.

What you want is for the dog to abandon that aggressive posture and relax. If it works, you can let the dogs interact again, but a bit farther apart than the first time and for a briefer duration. If the dogs do not warm up to each other within a few minutes, this is not a good fit.

Once you do find a shelter dog who seems to get along with Laddie, it is time

to see how they do at your home. Most shelters will agree to a trial period so that adoptive owners can make sure the new dog fits in with the family. Bring Laddie (and your friend) with you when you pick up the new dog, but separate the dogs during the car ride home, preferably in their own crates. Once you arrive home, take them both out of the car on leashes. Walk them a bit and see how they act before bringing them inside your home.

Support Laddie's position as the resident dog by bringing him into the house before your friend enters with the shelter dog. This gives a clear signal to the new dog that Laddie, at least for now, is the top dog. Once they become pals and the new dog feels comfortable in your home, the true dominant dog will emerge. It may be Laddie or the shelter dog. Top dog is always greeted first, fed first, and allowed to lead the other on walks.

Do not let the two dogs be off leash unsupervised until you are certain they get along. Dogs can hurt each other severely in fights. But from your description, Laddie sounds like a dog who will enjoy having a four-legged playmate. 🐾

TACTICS FOR A 12-LEGGED WALK

We just adopted a third dog, who quickly bonded with the other two. Now, every time I pick up a leash, all three get superexcited. How can I walk them at the same time without tangling the leashes and creating canine chaos?

Attempting to coordinate 12 furry legs desiring to move in three different directions can make choreographing a Broadway musical look like a cakewalk! It's good that your dogs are in sync with each other. Let's hope they move at about the same pace. If you can physically rein them in when necessary, then walking them all at once is feasible.

It's important to note that before you try to walk all three at once, each dog individually needs to know how to walk nicely on a leash. Once that is accomplished, walking the whole pack provides an opportunity to reinforce basic doggy commands and your status as leader of the pack.

The first thing to do is select a leash that doesn't tangle and cause you to trip. That means definitely not using retractable leashes, especially not with multiple dogs. I'm not a fan of these

zipline-type leashes because your dog can get so far ahead of you that you are no longer in control. If they pull the handles out of your hand or a line snaps, you could have dogs dashing off in different directions. Even if you do manage to hang on to all three, it's too easy for them to get entangled with each other or with a passing jogger or baby stroller.

Instead, opt for quality multidog walking leashes. My favorites include those with three-way couplers or two-way leashes that tether two dogs. In your other hand, you have a single leash for the third dog. Leashes should be six feet or less in length to give you control of your dogs' movements.

For walks around your neighborhood, arrange your dogs from left to right based on their temperaments. Place the most confident on the sidewalk closest to the street and the most unsure, cautious dog in the middle.

Ideally, you can load them all up in your vehicle and treat them to a fun walk in a dog-friendly park or the woods. There is less traffic, and you won't have to worry about navigating three dogs around neighborhood obstacles such as cars parked in driveways, sprinkler systems, or barking dogs lunging from front doors.

Keep an eye on your surroundings so you can spot possible hazards (squirrels in a tree, bicyclists, etc.) and adjust your route to minimize your dogs' possible reactivity. Finally, stay calm and maintain your leadership status by having your dogs practice synchronized sits—rewarded with small, healthy treats. With the right leash and the right attitude, team walking can be a breeze. 🐾

WANTED: A HAPPY CLOTHES HOUND

I love filling my walk-in closet with the latest fashion trends. I also love dogs, especially small ones. I am ready to adopt a puppy who will share my love for fashion. What are some ways I can encourage my new buddy to be a Fido fashionista?

Pet fashion is an ever-growing trend, with more than $350 million spent annually on pet Halloween costumes alone, according to the National Retail Federation. As we all bond closer with our dogs, more people are buying clothing and accessories for them. There is even a National Dress Up Your Pet Day—January 14!

Laurren Darr, founder of the International Association of Pet Fashion Professionals, reports that the trend is for more breed-specific attire and accessories as well as incorporating give-back missions. Dog fashion companies are teaming up with breed-specific rescue groups to stage dog fashion shows to get dogs adopted and showcase their products.

At the same time, pet apparel is moving from being simply cute to being highly functional. Shop smartly and safely. Look for fabrics that are light, breathable, and cooling or warming. Make sure the outfit does not contain any buttons, ribbons, or other pieces that can be swallowed and cause choking or gastrointestinal blockages. Avoid outfits that cover a dog's face or impair his vision. And make sure any canine clothing fits properly, without binding, pinching, or restricting movement.

In your quest to find a four-legged fashion lover, keep in mind that not every canine digs dressing up. My little Emma seems to strut when wearing her sweater on chilly days, but big Bujeau dashes out of the room when she sees me holding her sweater.

A dog who does not like being dressed up will let you know it. Some, like Bujeau, will try to hide before you can even get the outfit on them. If a dog won't move, sits or lies down, rolls frantically, or paws or bites at the clothing, it's a sure bet she isn't happy wearing clothes.

You are more likely to have success with a fashion-forward friend if you know your dog's personality. Confident, happy dogs who enjoy being handled and held and love greeting new people are more apt to be ideal candidates for

apparel. To accustom a dog to clothing, go slow and small. Try putting a doggy bowtie on your new pup and deliver praise and treats. Watch for her reaction. Once she's used to having things around her neck, slowly introduce her to other items of clothing, always starting with short sessions and praising her when she seems comfortable.

If your dog starts strutting her stuff, congratulations! You definitely have a delighted diva dog. If not, your pup may shine in another area that will make you just as proud while you take the fashion spotlight. 🐾

CASE OF CANINE ENVY

I have a whippet mix, Greta, and a border collie, Lex. Both are rescues that I adopted last year within a couple of months of each other. At best guess, Greta is about 3 and Lex is perhaps 4 years old. Whenever I rub Greta's belly or give her any special attention, Lex seems to appear out of nowhere and starts to paw at my arm or even let out a slight growl at Greta. Is Lex acting jealous? How can I give Greta some one-on-one time without Lex butting in?

You won't find *envy* in the canine dictionary, but the phrase *mine, mine, mine* certainly exists. Lex's behavior is triggered more by resource guarding than by jealousy over the attention Greta receives. Emma, my newest dog, is all of 9 pounds. During the first month

or so of her arrival, she would give a short, low growl any time one of the other cats or dogs wanted to cuddle with me on the couch.

As soon as she growled, I placed my index finger on the bridge of her nose—the location of the canine calming signal. (Momma dogs often place their mouths gently but firmly on that spot to get unruly puppies to settle down.) I then said, calmly, "No growl, Emma." If she growled a second time, I would place her on the floor. She quickly learned that growling at her older siblings cost her a precious spot on the couch. She now cuddles contentedly with anyone who joins us on the couch.

Watch closely the next time Greta and Lex play with a toy and you can identify clear canine communication. Chances are that one will body-block the other or lift an upper lip or make steady eye contact—signals that possession is nine-tenths of the law in the land of dogs. As hunters and pack animals, dogs have always demonstrated a "this is mine" attitude toward other canines when it comes to prized possessions, from the best part of the kill to a fuzzy chew toy.

When you rub Greta's belly, Lex steps in because he wants to guard the most valuable of all possessions—you. Fortunately, Lex's actions are meant to seek your attention, not to harm Greta, and Greta has not retaliated by reacting territorially. Left unchecked, however, this attention-seeking behavior might escalate and lead to tension, and perhaps even fights and injuries. I hope that no one is yelling or physically punishing either dog, because these actions heighten levels of stress and anxiety.

Take the time to train both your dogs to ban this resource-guarding mentality. Consider enrolling in a basic obedience course or refresher training class with them. Make sure the class uses positive, reward-based methods. At home, all members of the household need to reinforce the obedience rules and heed the game plan outlined below.

For a while, it might be necessary to separate the dogs when you want to devote individual time to each, by using doggy gates or putting one dog in a closed room or outside in a fenced backyard.

You should also teach Lex to *Go to your spot* whenever he approaches you when you are engaged in one-on-one time with Greta. (See Find Your Spot, Spot!, page 132.) This command can stop a fight from occurring because you, as leader of the pack, are giving Lex an activity to perform. Toss Lex a treat to reinforce this preferred, compliant behavior.

Most important, make sure you show Lex the same amount of attention so he doesn't feel that he needs to guard your time with him. Greta should also learn to wait quietly for attention in her own spot. 🐾

THE KIDS ARE BEGGING FOR A DOG

Our kids have been begging us to adopt a dog. My son is age 7 and my daughter is 9. They promise they will feed, walk, and play with the dog. Are they old enough to be responsible in caring for a dog? My husband and I both work. Should we say yes or wait?

Caring for dogs develops responsibility and self-esteem in children. By age 7, most children are mature enough to recognize that dogs, like people, have feelings and need kindness and care.

The actual skills necessary to care for pets, though, depend more on a child's ability to take responsibility and exercise self-control than on an age group. I know some 7-year-olds who are extremely attentive and capable of feeding, watering, exercising, and playing appropriately with puppies and dogs. I know some immature 12-year-olds who could not be trusted to feed a dog his daily meal even once.

You know your children's maturity levels. Spend some time with your spouse going over scenarios involving your children. Do they exercise proper caution by asking people if they can pet their dogs before bounding up to a dog? Do they complete their family chores on time? Do they take care of their toys? How do they act around pets belonging to friends and relatives?

You and your husband also need to ask questions of yourselves. Are you both willing to take on the added responsibilities and costs (in terms of time and money) of bringing a dog into the family? Are you willing to care for the dog when your children grow up and head for colleges or careers? Some dogs can live up to 18 years and longer. You could be caring for a senior dog with medical problems while your young adult children live hours away. Be candid with yourself and with each other.

Parents need to make canine care-giving an opportunity, not a punishment. If your son doesn't do his homework or your daughter forgets to take the garbage out, don't punish them by telling them they must now walk the dog. If caring for the dog feels like a burden, children may feel resentful or angry instead of loving and responsible.

Finally, round up your children for a family heart-to-heart talk. Remind them that dogs, unlike toys, are living, breathing animals with feelings. Then seek answers to the following questions.

- Why do you really want a dog? Because you love dogs or because you think you'll look cool around your friends?

- Are you willing to attend dog-training classes?

- Will you help feed, water, and exercise your dog every day?

- Will you not get mad if your puppy piddles in your room or chews your favorite book or accidentally scratches you when jumping up to greet you?

- Can you handle dog hair or drool on your clothes?

- Will you help bathe your dog and keep his bedding clean?

- Can you respect that your dog sometimes needs to be left alone, especially when napping or sleeping at night?

- Will you teach your dog commands and fun tricks?

- Will you obey leash laws when taking your dog out for walks?

- Are you willing to treat your dog with love and kindness?

Once you're satisfied with their responses, it is time to make this dog adoption truly a family affair. Teach children the right way to greet and respect the new family dog—and all dogs. Explain to them that when a dog tucks his tail, yelps, or tries to wiggle free from their bear hugs, these are signals to give your dog some space. Conversely, point out to your children that when their new dog approaches them freely and stays by them, these are positive signs that the dog enjoys their company.

After you adopt a dog, set up a schedule that lists who is doing which chore/activity each week for the new family dog. Put this schedule in a prominent place, perhaps on the refrigerator door, for easy access to check off completed tasks. A schedule can reduce the chances of forgetting to feed the dog or taking him for a needed walk. To ensure success, include your children in discussions on caring for your dog. Often, kids can offer some great suggestions and be part of the solution rather than part of the problem when it comes to solving behavior problems in your dog. 🐾

Choosing the Right Dog for a Child

Many of us are blessed with fond memories of our childhood dogs. Growing up in Indiana, I was lucky to pal with two dogs: Crackers, an overweight beagle, and Peppy, a high-energy border collie mix. Crackers moved quickly only when she smelled a plateful of food. Peppy behaved like a canine bar bouncer, swiftly ushering away any dog who dared to step a paw on our property.

Anytime you adopt a dog, but especially if you have young children, it's vital to do your homework about various breeds. The diverse dog world includes itty-bitty canines like the Chihuahua and the mountain-sized Saint Bernard. To some extent, purebreds possess certain temperaments—golden retrievers are accurately named for their sweet, sunny personalities—but there are always exceptions. I've met bashful Jack Russell terriers and boisterous Cavalier King Charles spaniels.

I tell you this so that you do not lock into a dog's breed as the sole indicator of temperament. Mixed-breed dogs also make wonderful pets. Remember that environment plays a keen part, too, in how dogs act and react. Dogs, like people, fill their brains with memories: good and bad, happy and scary. What happens to them as puppies can influence how they react to similar scenarios as adults.

In a household with children and working parents, where time is a precious commodity, my advice is to consider adopting a slightly older dog. A young adult dog most likely will have passed his chewing phase and will be house-trained and possibly have some basic obedience training. He will probably have received his puppy vaccinations and be neutered or spayed. Depending on the dog's personality and age, he could also be calmer than a high-spirited, got-to-explore-the-world-now puppy.

If you are interested in a particular breed, I suggest contacting a breed rescue group or other dog group that fosters adoptable dogs in family homes. You will get more details on the dog's personality and how he or she reacts to home settings—kids, adults, other pets, and even the vacuum cleaner.

CLINGY CANINE

Our sweet but insecure Australian shepherd came to us from a breed rescue group about a month ago. Louie follows us around the house like a shadow. When we come home from work, he always rushes to greet us and seems very anxious. Sometimes we find that he has shredded a sofa pillow or stolen the sponge from the kitchen and chewed it up.

We feel terrible leaving him alone, but we can't stay home 24 hours a day to keep him company, and we can't keep him in a crate all day either. What can we do to help him feel more at home when he is there by himself?

The biggest problems with dogs who are bored or anxious about being left at home include inappropriate elimination, incessant barking, and chewing up household items. Some dogs pace around in a panic or claw at windows and doors. Unless you win megamillions in the lottery and can suddenly quit your job, you can't change the fact that your dog spends more time inside your home than you do. Make sure he has a safe, cozy spot to hang out in during the day, and give him something fun to do in your absence.

You're right not to crate Louie if you are gone for more than four or five hours at a time. Crates are designed to be safe nesting areas for dogs, not prisons. No dog should be inside a crate for eight hours or more during the day. Instead, identify a room in your home where you can close a door or use doggy gates to keep Louie safely inside. These small places often give anxious dogs a feeling of security and may help him calm down. Make sure you thoroughly dog-proof any room where he will be spending time alone.

It is also important to avoid a common bad habit among working owners: making a big deal out of leaving and returning to your house. Start by rescripting your comings and goings. Some people unintentionally create separation anxiety in their dogs because they make a big deal of departures ("I'm so sorry I have to go work today, Max, you poor thing.") or arrivals ("Hey, Max! Guess who's home? Where's my sloppy kiss?"). For Louie's sake, cease the emotion-filled departures and arrivals.

Exit and enter without a lot of fanfare. Give him a treat or activity before you walk calmly out the door, but don't make a fuss about leaving. When you return, say hello, but then spend several

Breed Byte

Australian shepherds are touted for their ability to herd sheep and cattle, but this breed did not originate in the land down under. It actually got its start in California in the mid-nineteenth century.

minutes checking your mail or listening to your phone messages before making a fuss over him. You are teaching him that there's no need for a big production when you leave and return and that he must wait patiently for your undivided attention.

Here are a few other strategies to turn your home into a haven for Louie during your absence.

Wear him out. Make sure Louie gets plenty of exercise every day. Aussies are active dogs who have energy to burn. A good long walk or lively play session every morning will tire him out so he's more likely to nap than fret in your absence.

Bring on the feast. A few minutes before you head out the door for work, give Louie a hollow, hard rubber toy stuffed with his favorite treat: peanut butter, cream cheese, mashed bananas, pieces of rice cake, or some premium kibble. He should be so happily working at getting every little morsel that he won't notice your absence for hours. This tactic helps curb destructiveness, overeager greeting, and separation anxiety tendencies. Clean these rubber toys in your dishwasher or hot, soapy water at least once a week.

Provide some entertainment. Turn on the television or radio to provide some sound to counter the silence.

Vary the daily routine. If he likes other dogs, treat Louie to an occasional day at a doggy day care center or a mid-day visit from a dog-friendly neighbor or a professional pet sitter. (See Dial D for Doggy Day Care, page 165.)

Remember that Louie is a newcomer to your household and is still learning that he can trust you to come home every day. If you establish consistent routines and give him plenty of attention when you are at home, it won't be long before he feels like a full-fledged member of the family. 🐾

Does Your Dog Need Drugs?

Some dogs become so upset by their owner's absence that they break through windows, scratch up door frames, or destroy furniture in their frantic efforts to cope with feelings of abandonment. Dogs with serious separation anxiety issues may be too rattled to be distracted by food-filled toys or noise-muffling music and may need medication as well as behavior modification help from a professional behaviorist.

If you are dealing with a serious behavioral issue, you need solid guidance from someone properly trained to assist you and your dog. Look for a board-certified veterinary behaviorist (American College of Veterinary Behaviorists) or a certified-applied animal behaviorist. Ask for referrals from clients.

In those extreme cases, your veterinarian may refer you to a veterinary behaviorist trained to make an appropriate diagnosis and to choose the best behavioral medication, if necessary, to manage anxiety and distressed-based behavior problems. Be aware that some medications can take several weeks for dogs to show signs of improvement.

Although many of these medications are not addictive, efforts should be made to gradually wean a dog off the drug once he is stable and able to maintain his behavior through a combination of reduced doses and effective behavior modification. Some dogs may need to be on medication for their entire lives; others can function quite well on doses slowly reduced over time.

TRAINING CAN BE CHILD'S PLAY

We're planning on enrolling in a basic obedience class for our young border collie, Barney, and we hope to continue with clicker training and agility classes. My 10-year-old daughter is very interested in teaching Barney tricks. Is she too young to participate in the training classes with me? Will Barney respect her enough to obey her?

Many professional dog trainers report that their best students are children and teenagers. It makes sense. Children and puppies possess wonderful young minds that soak up learning like sponges. In dog-training classes, children learn success. They gain confidence by being able to show off tricks they taught their dog to their friends. It's definitely a win-win for dogs and for kids.

Children between the ages of 9 and 15 make the best students because they are the most open to learning. Adults often have too many bad habits to break or they become too goal-oriented. Trainers remark that it can be challenging to show adult students a new way to teach *Sit* and *Down*. The competitive nature also surfaces sometimes in classes with some adults wanting their dogs not only to learn the commands but also to be the best. That puts undue pressure on a dog.

Another plus for young students: great hand-eye coordination and timing. In clicker training, you learn to press a small metal device to make a clicking sound each time your dog does the right step. You immediately follow that sound with a small treat to reinforce his actions. The timing of the click is essential. Adults may be a little slow with the clicking sound, but children possess good hand-eye coordination, thanks in part to their video game skills. They usually manage to click on cue.

I know a 9-year-old named Kim who enrolled in a clicker-training puppy class with her dachshund puppy, Bogart. The trainer in charge told me that Kim ranked top in her class, which included mostly adults. Kim even surprised her mom by getting Bogart to heed basic commands like *Sit*, *Stay*, and *Find your spot* during the first day of clicker-training class. Now Kim and Bogart have advanced to work on new commands and fun tricks, and their confidence levels rise with each success.

Your children represent the next generation of the pet-loving public, so encourage them to join you in your dog's training classes. Then sit back and witness the maturity growth in both your children and your dog. 🐾

AND BABY MAKES FOUR

My husband and I jokingly refer to Samson as our first child. We adopted him from a greyhound rescue organization two years ago; he is now 4. Samson is sweet, gentle, and charming with people. I just found out that I'm pregnant. We're excited about having a baby, but what should we do to prepare Samson for the new arrival? We don't want him to be jealous or upset.

Congratulations on becoming a parent—again! Samson's sweet temperament should make for an easy transition upon the arrival of your baby. Still, he will surely be curious, and while a dog won't feel jealous the way an older sibling might, he may feel the need to compete with this new addition for your time and attention.

Start now to prepare Samson by gradually spending less one-on-one time with him. This is not meant to be unkind but to help him cope with your need to devote a lot of time and energy to caring for your baby. If you are Samson's primary caregiver, have your husband take over some of those duties. You want Samson to continue to feel he is loved and a vital member of the family but not that he is the central focus of your attention. You also don't want him to feel neglected.

Before the baby arrives, introduce Samson to as many other infants and toddlers as possible. Invite friends who have babies to visit so that Samson becomes accustomed to little ones in the house. Take him for walks near playgrounds or schools. Play videos or recordings of babies and children. Look for any opportunity to expose Samson to the sights, sounds, and smells of the baby world: crying, babbling, diaper changing, strollers, and so forth. You're building him a baby database that he can download when your baby comes home.

Of course, it is very important that you closely supervise his interaction with all babies and children. Reward him for gentle behavior, and correct him if he is too nosy or if he tries to lick them. Teach him to sit politely to be petted. Be aware that sighthounds might chase and knock down running children, whose erratic

motion and high-pitched voices can trigger chasing instincts. Don't take the chance of any child getting accidentally injured or bitten by a dog who feels defensive or who becomes too excited.

Silly as it sounds, I recommend that you carry a baby doll around with you when you walk Samson and when you relax to read or watch television with him in the room. Get a recording of baby sounds and play it. A friend of mine even sprinkled baby powder on her forearm and put baby food on her fingers to get her dog used to those new smells.

Before the baby comes home, ask your husband or a friend to bring Samson a blanket or other object that smells of your baby for him to sniff and become familiar with. When you and the baby first come home, make the initial introduction a rewarding one. Enter the house alone and give Samson a happy greeting and treat. Then have your husband follow with the baby. Give Samson plenty of time to sniff and look over the baby while you keep a close watch on them.

Your life is about to change drastically, and many of your usual routines will be altered or gone forever. However busy you are, though, try to spend some quality solo time each day with Samson—even just a few minutes will help him feel more secure. No matter how much you trust him, however, always supervise him when he is with the baby. With careful preparation and continued attention, Samson should quickly learn to accept this new addition to the pack and still feel loved by you and your husband. 🐾

SMALL DIGS, BIG DOG

I live on the tenth floor of a high-rise building in New York City. My one-bedroom condo is 600 square feet. I love city life and don't plan to move, but I really want to adopt a dog. I volunteer at a doggy day care on Saturdays, and I know that I could offer a deserving dog a good home. I prefer larger dogs, ones that weigh at least 50 pounds. Would living in such a small space drive a big dog crazy?

By all means, adopt a big, lovable dog, but choose carefully. Physical size does not necessarily parallel the amount of energy a dog possesses. Some of the top canine couch loungers include greyhounds and Great Danes. Conversely, some dogs that turn into interior designers of the worst kind (chewing rugs and

and smells. These exposures usually enhance their social skills when they meet people and other critters during daily walks. Most big cities offer numerous canine amenities like doggy spas, bakeries, day cares, training centers, and dog-friendly transportation. When I visit New York City, I love seeing people sharing the back seats of taxis with their well-behaved large dogs. I even had a few cabbies remark that dogs often have better manners than some of their two-legged riders!

Big cities also provide plenty of places for dogs to get exercise. Seek out dog-friendly parks and canine play groups. If you work all day, look into a doggy day care or hire a professional dog walker to give your dog a break in the middle of the day.

Don't let the size of your place stop you from teaching your dog city manners. Keep plenty of treats in your tiny kitchen and work on commands like *Sit pretty* (ideal when sharing elevators with dog-apprehensive strangers) and *Curb* (stopping and sitting at intersections until the light turns green).

Your dog will be happy to demonstrate his repertoire of tricks during walks and perhaps the two of you will convert more New Yorkers into dog fans. And, of course, don't forget to scoop your poop! 🐾

shredding sofas, while yapping nonstop) weigh in at less than 15 pounds.

Before you take any steps toward adopting, though, check with your condo association and learn their pet rules. Savvy condo groups focus on temperament—not poundage—in their pet policies. They want well-behaved dogs and responsible owners. Your next step should be to honestly assess how much time you have to exercise a dog and then be careful to choose a canine companion that will be satisfied with what you provide.

In other words, if you can walk a dog twice a day for only 15 minutes, don't get a high-energy breed that needs lots of exercise. Great Danes, for example, are not typically shoving a leash in your lap and beckoning you to the door to run a marathon every day.

Dogs are very adaptable, and city dogs are exposed to many sights, sounds,

DIAL D FOR DOGGY DAY CARE

Lately, I've found myself spending more and more time at my job, leaving early in the morning and sometimes not coming home until around 7 p.m. I share my home with my wonderful dog, Murphy. He is 4 years old and well behaved. He likes other dogs and loves helping me entertain when we have company. He has access to a dog door to my side yard during the day, and I leave him with toys and snacks and water.

When I walk in the door, Murphy is ready to play, but I am exhausted. I feel guilty that I can't give him the attention and exercise he deserves. He is beginning to chew things and beg for constant attention at night. What can I do?

Guilt is a human emotion not a canine one. I came up with the acronym GUILT (Great, Useful, Intelligent, Loving Tactics) for working out solutions to problems like juggling a demanding job and a young, playful dog. First of all, recognize that you're exhausted and your dog is frustrated. Murphy sounds like a sweet dog who enjoys your company, but you are right to be worried that he needs more attention. You've done a good job in providing him with the basic amenities, but the 12-hour days are cutting into quality time for you and Murphy and reducing his opportunities to exercise.

My suggestion is that you treat Murphy to doggy day care a couple of days a week. Many places offer quality care with hours that match your schedule. Don't let the price dissuade you. A young, energetic dog left home alone all day can start to display signs of loneliness and boredom, including destructive chewing, nonstop barking, and inappropriate urination. Correcting these bad behaviors and repairing the damage done by the dog can cost you more time and money (and much more frustration) than you will pay for day care.

Murphy will enjoy unleashing his pent-up energy and hanging out with canine pals. At the end of the workday, you will pick up a tired, happy dog, not one who's been eagerly awaiting your return all day and is dying to play. You can come home and relax with your dog before heading for bed. You both win.

Another option is to hire a professional pet sitter, a person who is trained, licensed, and insured, to come once a day to take Murphy for a leashed walk. Trust your dog in the hands of a pet sitter rather than try to save a few dollars

Choosing a Good Day Care

In deciding which doggy day care is best for your dog, ask your canine-owning friends to tell you what they like and don't like about area doggy day cares. If there are several choices, narrow down your list to the most appealing ones and call to schedule a visit—alone. Taking your dog on your initial visit will only distract you and keep you from conducting an objective assessment.

At each doggy day care, follow this checklist.

○ **Take a complete tour of the center.** Staff members at quality centers are happy to show prospective clients where dogs play, lounge, and rest. Scratch off centers where staff members refuse to show the entire place.

○ **Size up the facility.** Look at the number and size of dogs, and determine if the space allocated is adequate or too small. Make sure the center offers a safe, enclosed outdoor area.

○ **Ask about the ratio of staff to dogs.** Well-run establishments should have one employee for every four to six dogs. Dogs should never be left unsupervised.

○ **Check for cleanliness.** Accidents happen, but good centers quickly clean up messes. Use your ears and nose, too. You shouldn't be deafened by the sound of noisy barking, and the place should smell fresh and clean.

○ **Review the admission policy.** Responsible centers require that all doggy guests be up-to-date on their vaccinations, be on regular flea and tick maintenance programs, be spayed or neutered, and be nonaggressive.

Once you've chosen a place, pay attention to your dog's reaction to attending doggy day care. If he enjoys his time there, he will usher you to the door when he is dropped off instead of resisting and yanking the leash in the opposite direction. He should be happy to see you when you pick him up at the end of the workday but not desperate to leave and acting anxious and nervous.

by having a teenager or retiree in your neighborhood walk Murphy.

Pet sitters are trained on how to handle dogs on walks to reduce the risk of a dog bite incident or other issue. They also are trained to spot any issues in the dogs to report back to their clients. You may find that Murphy regards this pet sitter as a favorite "aunt" or "uncle" and looks forward to these regular outings. To locate a reputable professional pet sitter, check out the two main organizations: the National Association of Professional Pet Sitters and Pet Sitters International. 🐾

CASE OF THE SHRINKING BED

I live with three big dogs who range in weight from 85 to 160 pounds. One drools. They are all males, ages 3 to 6. They are very sweet, but their size seems to scare off potential boyfriends; that and the fact that all three of them sleep in my queen-sized bed with me. Obviously, there is very little room for even me!

How can I find a great mate who isn't intimidated—or turned off—by my canine trio? How can I get my canine trio to accept a serious boyfriend in my bedroom?

Sounds like you want a guy who loves dogs but doesn't act like one! Use the fact that you love your three dogs to your advantage in the dating game. Surveys show that people who own dogs are perceived as nice and kind.

You have several options. Consider joining one of the growing number of pet-friendly online dating services. Hang out at your local dog park and strike up conversations with guys. Offer to volunteer at a fundraising event for a local shelter or rescue group. Look for a "yappy hour" in your area (but take only one dog at a time!).

The key to finding a guy who shares your love for dogs is to be honest. Let guys know right up front that you share your home with three large dogs. In searching for a mate, don't sacrifice your beliefs and certainly don't dismiss the needs of your dogs. Steer clear of any guy who tells you to decide between him and your dogs. Those "me or the dog" guys aren't worth your time or energy.

Dating Goes to the Dogs

The world is changing rapidly, and one sign of the times is that pets are commanding more attention in many human relationships. About 62 percent of US households have pets. Of those, about 40 million are single people. There are websites for people with pets looking for mates who have pets or at least like them.

A national survey conducted by a leading pet product manufacturer reported that a majority of dog owners would stop dating someone who didn't like their dog or if their dog didn't like the date.

Dating issues aside, I strongly recommend you train your canine pals to sleep in their own beds in your bedroom. Pets are definitely one of those environmental factors such as sound, temperature, humidity, light, and movement that contribute to poor sleep. Researchers at the Mayo Clinic Sleep Disorders Center have discovered that about half the people who let pets share their bed at night suffer from disrupted sleep that results in being tired each morning.

Initially, you need to make your bed less inviting. You could try covering your bed with sheets of bubble wrap or another crinkly material that sounds and feels unappealing to your dogs. You won't win any bedroom décor awards, but this is a temporary measure. Provide each of them with a comfy canine bed in your room and train them to go to their spots (see page 132).

As for introducing another human to your room, make sure your canine trio meets your boyfriend outside the bedroom first. Let them spend some time getting treats from him and playing with him. Bonding with and building trust in him will help your dogs to feel okay about him being in any room in your house. 🐾

POODLE HOGS PILLOW

My poodle, Precious, earns her name, at least during daylight hours. She is sweet, gentle, and always ready to learn new tricks. My problem is that she turns into a pillow pig at night. She starts out by putting her head on the edge of my pillow, but by the middle of the night, she has taken over half or more. Her activity wakes me up. Sometimes she presses her cold, wet nose against my neck or emits little yips when she is deep in dreamland. I want her to sleep on my bed, but how can I keep her off my pillow so I can get some sleep?

When it comes to sharing your bed with your dog, you're not alone. About one-third of today's dog owners sleep with their pets. The term *three-dog night* might have originated in Alaska or Australia or Siberia, but wherever it came from it refers to adding dogs as bed warmers based on the temperature. The colder the night, the more dogs. Three dogs would be enough to keep your toes toasty.

Precious sounds like one bossy poodle. She has decided that bedtime entitles her to sleep wherever she chooses, regardless of your preferences. Cute as she may be, you need to regain control of your bed, not only to enjoy a sound sleep but also to remind Precious who calls the shots. You are fortunate that she has not become territorial about bedtime turf. Some dogs who view themselves as top dogs in the family will growl or even nip their human mates who dare to toss and turn at night.

It's time to teach Precious that although she is welcome on your bed, you are the one who determines where she sleeps. Make her sit and wait until you call her up. Direct her to the foot of your bed and provide her with her own pillow or special blanket. If she ventures north toward your pillow, move her back to the foot of the bed. Once she is there, praise her. It may take a few nights before Precious learns your new bedtime rules, but eventually she will roost in her own spot and let you enjoy a full night's sleep without a pillow fight. 🐾

Breed Byte

The Mexican hairless breed, also known as the xoloitzcuintli, was valued by pre-Aztec Mexicans as a bed warmer and companion.

Barking with the Big Dogs

Small dogs are gaining in popularity, but big dogs still rule. According to the American Kennel Club, the five most popular breeds are the Labrador retriever, French bulldog, German shepherd, golden retriever, and bulldog. Itty-bitty dogs rank 6th with the toy poodle and 13th with the Yorkshire terrier.

MINE, MINE, ALL MINE

Our French bulldog, Foggy, has started to growl and snap at our cats whenever they come within 10 feet of his food bowl, even if it is empty. Recently, he lunged at one of them, forcing her to flee up a cat tree to escape. He also stares icily at my husband and me when we walk by his bowl. Foggy is 9 months old and neutered. When the food bowl isn't involved, he is fun and friendly and obedient. Why is he guarding his food bowl with such intensity?

Foggy doesn't hold the deed to your house or the title to your car, but he does know the concept of ownership. From his viewpoint, the food bowl—empty or full—is one of his most prized possessions and, even if they show no interest in it, he must ensure that cats or people don't attempt to steal his bowl.

This common type of resource guarding harks back to his ancestors' need to protect food and other resources in order to survive. Snapping and growling at other members of the pack was a way for dogs to tell them to back off and leave their food alone. Despite being domesticated, some modern-day dogs extend this territorial thinking to favorite toys, bedding, and even a particular location in the house, like a sunny spot near a window.

At 9 months, Foggy is beginning to feel more grown-up, and like all young adults, he is testing the limits of authority. He wants to know if he can chase you away from his bowl and if the cats will yield to his threats. From your description, Foggy's turf defending is growing in intensity and range. Unchecked, this behavior can escalate from growls and lunging to snapping or even to biting.

As natural as it may seem, do not yell at Foggy or physically punish him for guarding his food bowl. You risk only making the problem worse: He will feel a greater need to protect his bowl since it will appear to him that you are angry enough to fight for it.

This problem did not surface overnight, and it won't go away in one day. It takes time to stop resource guarding. The first step is to establish a new dinnertime protocol. You and your husband must call the shots at meals. Your goal is to teach Foggy that positive experiences occur when people approach his bowl and that you reign as the Keeper of Great Chow, worthy of his respect.

Do not let Foggy be a free feeder who nibbles all day. Take his bowl away between meals and store it out of sight. During your retraining period, bring out not one but two food bowls—one empty and one containing food. Call the dog to a new feeding place that isn't a high-traffic area in your home. Moving the bowl into different locations at mealtimes will reduce Foggy's territorial tendencies.

Place the bowls on a counter or shelf out of his reach. Ask Foggy to *Sit* and *Stay* and then put down the empty bowl. (Watch the surprised look on his face!) Then drop a piece of food into the empty bowl on the ground. Do not bend over. Wait until he eats that piece before dropping another. If he shows no protectiveness, try putting a few pieces of food in your hand and invite him to take them.

Alternate between dropping food in his bowl and hand-feeding him. When he starts to eat from his bowl, drop more pieces into it. Once in a while, drop in a "jackpot treat" like a piece of chicken or steak, something that ranks far higher in value than his regular dog food. It may take several meals before he accepts this new method of dining.

Once Foggy shows no signs of tension, you're ready for the next phase. Partially fill one bowl with his food and place it on the floor. Call Foggy and again have him *Sit* and *Stay* before you allow him to approach his food bowl. The goal is to make him work for his food.

As he starts to eat, place a second bowl with some premium food about

build positive associations and increase Foggy's trust that you, or other people, will make feeding time fun and exciting, not tense and upsetting.

You are using positive reinforcement rather than threats or physical force to show Foggy that food time is not a time to fight. He is learning that by giving up a resource, he earns something even better. Eventually, you will be able to present him with a single bowl, though he should always be expected to sit and wait for your signal before eating.

When I followed these steps with my corgi, Jazz, his guarding behavior disappeared within a couple of weeks. We turned mealtime into a fun game of doggy dining etiquette. He would happily leap into a *Sit* position, watch me put down the bowl, heed my *Wait* cue and my *Watch me* cue before approaching his bowl once I gave the *Okay* sign. I was able to pet his back while he ate, praising him. It worked with Jazz, and it can work for you and Foggy.

If your efforts are not successful, however, I urge you to seek help from a professional animal behaviorist. Resource guarding is a serious behavior problem that can eventually threaten the safety of you and your cats, as well as your family and visitors. 🐾

10 feet away. Call him over to this bowl. As he starts to eat from the second bowl, go back to the first bowl and add special treats to up its food value before you call Foggy over. Continue switching between bowls until he has finished his meal, then take them away and hide them.

Over a few weeks, gradually bring the two bowls closer together as you feed him. You need to watch Foggy's reactions to determine how quickly you can merge the two bowls. He should be displaying a relaxed body posture. This dual-bowl tactic is designed to

RUFF! RUFF! ROAD TRIP!

All I have to do is say the words "car ride" and my Labrador retriever gets giddy with excitement and starts dancing around. I enjoy taking him along when I go on errands and when I visit family and friends out of town. He absolutely loves to ride in the front seat and stick his head out the window. Why do so many dogs like to do this? I'm a conscientious driver, but is there anything I can do to make life on the road with my dog safer?

Be happy that he isn't begging for the keys like a teenager! Many dogs love car rides, and one reason is that they exist in a world of smells. The canine nose acts like a steering wheel, directing dogs from one great odor to the next.

As they whiz along with their heads out the window, dogs are gathering in a wealth of information about the passing world. Road trips also help hone canine socialization skills by exposing dogs to new and different sights, sounds, and, most important, smells with each passing mile.

As much as we might enjoy their company in the front seat, dogs are safer sitting in the back, where they can't distract the driver and won't be injured by airbags in an accident. Just as children have car seats and adults use seat belts, our dogs also need to be safely confined inside a moving vehicle. There are a variety of products for canine car comfort available in pet stores and pet supply catalogs. Depending on the size of your dog and your vehicle, you should consider crates or canine seatbelts to prevent canine free rein. Station wagons can be fitted with grates to keep your passenger in the back compartment.

All three of my dogs love car trips, even if it is just to join me when I pick up lunch at a drive-through window. But all it takes is a sudden stop for an untethered dog to become a projectile inside your car, possibly injuring you both. For their safety, my dogs ride in harnesses in the back seat. The larger two, 35-pound Kona and 90-pound Bujeau, sit on dog beds with special straps that snap into the seatbelt buckles. They can move around but are not able to jump into the front seat.

Little Emma, all of 9 pounds, is tethered in an elevated canine booster basket where she can safely look out the window. Some dogs can develop motion sickness if they are unable to see out the windows. I keep the windows up or cracked open just a bit. A dog who is able to stick his head out an opened window is at risk of leaping out or getting eye injuries from flying debris.

A final safety tip: Always put your dog's leash on before you open the door to prevent him from bolting out and getting hurt in traffic or lost. This is the ideal setting to reinforce the *Wait* cue. 🐾

ON THE ROAD WITH ROVER

My husband and I are retired, and we have always wanted to trek cross-country by car. We're planning to drive to a family reunion in Maine from our home in Oregon. We want to take the time to enjoy this country from coast to coast, and we want to take our fox terrier, Sammy, with us. He loves to ride in the car and is well behaved. Do you have any advice for finding pet-friendly hotels and tips for traveling with dogs?

Fortunately, there is an increasingly wide range of lodgings, from the inexpensive to the luxurious, that are putting out the welcome mat for doggy guests. Over the past few years, my dogs and I have stayed in bargain-priced motels and oh-so-canine-fine hotels with doggy spas. Some places offer dog-walking services and doggy day care. At one fancy resort, Kona was treated to a two-hour guided hike, followed by a pet massage and bath—she loved the attention!

The fact that you are not in a hurry, and that Sammy is a seasoned, well-mannered traveler, can make your trip truly memorable. My first piece of advice is to heed the Golden Rule of Traveling: Never try to sneak your dog into a hotel that doesn't permit pets. You risk losing a night's fee as a penalty and after a full day of driving, you may be unable to find another, more accommodating option nearby.

If you belong to AAA or another motorist organization, stop by the local office for a book listing pet-friendly hotels. There are also several websites that identify lodgings that accept canine guests (see Useful Websites, page 214). Chat with your friends who travel with their dogs and ask them for recommendations. When booking, ask the hotel if they have special pet rooms and what the pet deposit fee is. Some are refundable, but some are not.

If possible, request a room on the first floor away from high-traffic areas.

Find out where you can take Sammy for his bathroom needs and what the cleanup requirements are.

Bring along a small sign to hang on the doorknob or front of the door to alert the housekeeping staff that Sammy is inside. Some places provide customized privacy signs that notify visitors that one of the guests inside has four legs, but bring your own just in case. (See Travel Tips for Rover, page 177, for a list of other items to bring along.)

No matter how well behaved he is at home, Sammy must not be allowed free rein inside the room unsupervised. When you and your husband go to dinner or check out a tourist attraction, leave him in a crate with all his creature comforts (water, favorite chew toy, and bedding) and turn the television or radio on at a low volume to muffle hallway sounds. Never leave him in a crate for more than a few hours. Another option is to bring a portable gate that keeps him safely in the bathroom area and set up a cozy spot for him there.

When you take Sammy out of your room, he needs to be on his best behavior. When you are at the front desk, put him in a *Sit-Stay*. That simple obedience cue wows the staff and generates positive comments from other guests. A dog who is friendly and well behaved will usually become a favorite with staff and guests alike, especially if he performs a couple of cool tricks as well.

Finally, always tidy up as you prepare to check out and leave the housekeeping staff a nice tip. These gestures create a positive impression that will benefit other pet lovers desiring to travel with their canine chums. 🐾

TRAVEL FEAR: LOST DOG

We sold our home and bought an RV to realize our dream of exploring the country. Joining us is Leo, our medium-sized dog. He loves to travel and is friendly to everyone. He knows our neighborhood, but what should I do if he happens to dart out the RV door and get lost?

This is a common concern among those in the growing RV community as well as those who take their dogs with them on vacations. Fortunately, the RV community rallies around pets, and there is a lot of information available online about traveling safely with pets. In addition, there are groups who specialize in helping pet parents find missing dogs, such as the CT Dog Gone Recovery Volunteers and Lost Dogs of America. Contact them immediately should Leo dash away.

Here are some dos and don'ts when traveling with your dog to reduce the chances of them disappearing.

- Do make sure Leo is wearing a collar with visible ID tags and has been microchipped with your cell phone number.

- Do train Leo ahead of time to come when called.

- Do keep photos of Leo on your smartphone in different poses and have printed copies on hand that you can quickly share with those in the RV park area.

- Do leave highly aromatic food out for your dog. Put it in a safe spot close to your RV.

- Do enlist the help of people to spread out and search and instruct them to alert you of Leo's whereabouts but not try to grab him. Lost dogs are not likely to trust strangers. If anyone has a drone to survey from above, even better.

- Don't scream and give chase. Most dogs will run faster and farther away.

- Don't simply put up signs in the area and post photos online. Give details for identifying him and directions that might be helpful: "Leo is very shy, so please don't chase him or try to grab him. If you can, please take a picture that will help us pinpoint his location." Use social media: Post photos and details on Facebook, Twitter, or whatever channels you use. Ask people to repost to spread the word.

Most important, don't give up! 🐾

Sniff It Out!

Some of the best dog addresses in North America include Bark River, Michigan; Bassett, California; Yorkshire, New York; and of course the Canadian provinces of Labrador and Newfoundland.

Travel Tips for Rover

If you frequently take your dog with you in the car, keep a kit with doggy travel essentials in your trunk. My must-have list includes a water bowl, bottled water, an extra leash and a collar with identification tags, poop bags, an old towel, premoistened wipes, a basic first-aid kit, necessary medications, a copy of health records, bedding, treats, and at least a one-day supply of food.

During your trip, watch for any signs of motion sickness, dehydration, or other health issues. On a long drive, stop every couple of hours to let your dog stretch, have a drink, relieve himself, and move around for a few minutes.

Most important, pay attention to the weather. You've heard it before, but the facts are frightening: Dogs left inside cars during the summer can suffer from heat exhaustion and die within minutes, even with the windows open. When you are driving, turn on the air conditioner when temperatures start to sizzle and make sure the vents are directing cool air to the back seat.

TABLE FOR TWO, PLEASE

When the weather is nice, a lot of cafés in my town have outdoor seating, and they allow dogs if they are on leashes and behave nicely. My dog, Max, listens to me, but I often observe rude behavior by other dogs who are out of control. What can I do to avoid people whose dogs shouldn't be allowed in public?

You have unleashed a topic that brings out the barker in me. Outdoor eateries offer dogs the chance to show off good manners and to hang out with you instead of being stuck at home. Unfortunately, the percentage of eateries that permit dogs is shrinking because of the failure of dog owners to exercise some basic dining etiquette. Restaurant managers don't want dogs who yap, wrestle, or roam freely from table to table—it's bad for business.

You can't control your environment entirely, but you can take steps to heighten the chance of enjoying a pleasant dining experience with Max in tow. Here are some tips.

Tire him out. Treat Max to some aerobic exercise before you head for the café so that he is more apt to nap

under the table while you dine. This also gives him the chance to take a bathroom break before you are ready to sit down and order.

Try to dine during off-peak times, such as mid-morning and late afternoon. Weekdays are usually quieter than weekends.

Rein in your dog. Keep Max on a four- to six-foot leash tethered to your chair leg. Make sure he is not able to reach other tables to practice his begging skills.

Request a table in an out-of-the-way corner. Dogs like to have a view in front of them and a wall behind them to prevent anyone from sneaking up on them.

Pack his lunch. If the restaurant does not have a doggy menu, bring Max a healthy treat or a chew toy and a portable collapsible water bowl.

Resist the temptation to have Max meet and greet other dining dogs. Introductions should be saved for after mealtime and should take place in a spacious, public place. Politely let intrusive owners know of your wishes.

If you forget your dog's bowl, politely request a water bowl for your dog (with ice, if she prefers it that way!).

Leave a generous tip—the waiter will remember and be more apt to accommodate you and Max on your next visit. Bone appetite! 🐾

CHECK YOUR DOG FROM HEAD TO TAIL

I love my dog, Freddy, so much. He is the first dog I've had as an adult and, boy, did I get lucky! He is friendly to everyone he meets and never has accidents in the house. I take him for twice-a-year veterinary exams and he gets top-quality food. What else can I do to keep him at his healthy best? I really look forward to being together for many years.

Freddy is one lucky dog to be with you, too! He sounds like a genuine "heart dog" who will make you smile fur-ever. So Freddy deserves a real treat from you—one that is calorie-free but full of healthy goodies. In my pet first-aid classes, I love teaching people how to be their pets' best health allies by performing a head-to-tail wellness check that all pet owners can do weekly. Kona loves this part of the class, too, because she is treated to a purposeful massage and garners lots of attention from the students.

These at-home inspections offer the opportunity for you and Freddy to bond even closer. They also mean you can find potential health issues early on, when it may be easier and less costly to address them. Weekly exam sessions also condition Freddy that hands are friends, not foes, meaning he will be more receptive to being touched during a veterinary exam or during a grooming session. Win-win-win!

Pick a quiet room in your house and at a time when you can focus without distractions for about 10 minutes. Here's the routine.

Head. Hold a treat in front of his eyes and move it back and forth slowly to make sure his eyes can track the treat and that he doesn't wince or show limited mobility in his neck. Look at his eyes to make sure that they are clear and free of any discharge.

Nose and ears. Gently touch his nose. A healthy dog's nose can be dry or slightly moist. An unhealthy nose might be full of mucus or extremely dry and cracked. Sniff and look inside each ear. There shouldn't be any dirty-sock smell or dark brown dirt that looks like coffee grounds—a sign of ear mites.

Paws. Pick up each paw, looking and feeling for any cuts, tenderness, or redness. Inspect the nails to make sure they are not overgrown, and gently spread the toes apart to check for ticks—this yucky check should be done daily in tick season.

Tail. Glide your hand down his tail to check for any cuts or bumps. Raise the tail and check the back end to make sure there is no dried urine or poop dangling or swollen anal glands.

Coat and skin. Take a good look at Freddy's coat to make sure that it is shiny and clean and not oily or shedding excessively. The skin is the largest organ; if it is looks poor, there may be something going on healthwise that warrants a veterinary visit.

Body check. Finally, have Freddy sit as you position yourself behind him and glide the palm of your open hand from his head to the base of the tail. Then take your fingertips and slowly and gently massage his whole body. You are looking for any cuts, hot spots, signs of parasites, hard masses, skin growths, or wincing that may mean a sore muscle. Praise your dog calmly at the end.

Be sure to let your veterinarian know if you find anything out of the ordinary so it can be treated before the condition worsens. 🐾

Ah, There's the Rub

Who doesn't love a good massage? The purposeful kneading and pressing and circular motion help loosen muscle knots, unleash tension, and increase blood flow and range of motion in all sorts of creatures. A nice massage not only warms body tissues and removes toxins and wastes from the body, it also conditions your dog to being touched, improves socialization, and bolsters your friendship bond.

You can book an appointment for your dog with a licensed pet massage therapist—or you can learn how to perform a therapeutic dog massage yourself. Here are the basic steps.

- Pick a quiet place free of distractions and temptations so your dog can focus on your healing hands and fully enjoy the experience. Allow your dog to get into her favorite position: sitting or lying down on her side.

- Never use massage oils. Clean your hands before you begin.

- Use your hands and fingertips, not your nails, to make slow, deliberate movements. An easy position is the open hand. With your palm facing down, apply gentle pressure in long, flowing strokes from your dog's head to tail. Another easy stroke is called "finger circles." Use the tips of your fingers and make small, tight circles on your dog's muscles in clockwise and counterclockwise directions.

- Pay attention to your dog's feedback signs. Continue if he is relaxed, and stop when he becomes restless.

Check with local veterinary clinics or animal shelters to find a canine massage class near you. I promise it will be one of the most fun and beneficial classes you've ever attended. But your dog shouldn't be the only one in your household getting massages. Book a monthly appointment with a massage therapist and treat yourself!

TURN HO-HUM INTO HOORAY!

I know it is important to walk my dog every day, but it is boring. I sense that Tippy, my corgi, is bored, too. We walk around our neighborhood for about 20 minutes twice a day. Tippy smells the same mailboxes, the same grass, the same car tires. I know that dogs like routines, but what can we do to break out of this monotony and make walks more interesting and fun?

Dogs live by the motto "So Many Smells, So Little Time." In Tippy's case, he surely can tell you every single scent that is within your 20-minute range, so it's time for new frontiers. Start by varying your routes, the duration of your walks, and, if possible, the time of day that you walk. Simply switching to the other side of the street will introduce Tippy to a bonanza of new sights, sounds, and smells.

Invite a friend with a friendly dog who likes Tippy to join you on your walks. Having company will liven up the routine for both of you. If your weekday walks must follow your work schedule, take time on the weekends to drive Tippy to a pet-friendly place for a longer hike. Or treat him to playtime at a local dog park if he is friendly with other dogs.

Daily walks provide golden opportunities for you to reinforce basic obedience training and introduce new tricks. Unleash some fun, creative ways to bust boredom on your regular treks with my four favorite walking games: the Molasses Walk, the Jackrabbit Sprint,

Park It Here, and Curbside Attraction. Your increased activity may evoke some giggles and stares from onlookers, so bring your sense of humor with you on the walks. Act goofy and it will be contagious to Tippy and others.

The Molasses Walk begins with Tippy walking nicely at your side with the leash loose. Ask Tippy to look at you as you take giant steps forward in slow motion saying "s-l-o-w" in a drawn-out way. The goal is for Tippy to copy your slow stride. When he does, reward him with praise (*Good slow!*) and a treat. Continue doing this slow walk for 10 or 15 seconds and then return to a normal pace.

The Jackrabbit Sprint is designed to pick up the pace. Start power walking and in an exuberant tone tell Tippy to go fast, fast, fast, fast! (Don't move so quickly that you are dragging him behind you, though!) Keep this pace up for 10 or 15 seconds and then stop. Give him a treat and a word of praise and resume your normal walk.

Park It Here spices up walks with a fun activity. Depending on the size of your dog and his physical condition, pick a park bench or sturdy low surface onto which he can easily jump. Train Tippy by tapping your hand on the bench, then making a sweeping up motion as you say, *Jump up!* Help him initially by hoisting him up if he seems confused by this strange request. Once he is on the bench, make him sit for a few seconds before giving him permission to leap off. Praise and treat and be on the lookout for the next bench Tippy can conquer.

The Curbside Attraction trick makes crossing a not-too-busy street more interesting. With Tippy facing you on the sidewalk, stand on the street (very close to the curb, so you don't risk getting hit by a car). Ask him to *Sit*, and then use a treat to slowly lure him forward—the idea is have him move just his front feet.

As soon as his front legs touch the street and his back legs remain on the curb, reinforce the pose by saying "curb." At the same time, put your open hand in front of his face to stop him from continuing to move forward into the street. Praise and treat. This looks quite comical, but dogs have a sense of humor, too.

These are just a few suggestions for spicing up your walks. If you vary your routine and make up your own fun games, I'm sure both you and Tippy will enjoy your daily outings more. 🐾

NOT A GYM GROUPIE

I confess. I am a germophobe. I always carry a bottle of hand sanitizer with me, I avoid handshakes, and I cringe when someone near me sneezes. I want to stay in shape but do not feel safe inside a sweaty gym, and my apartment is way too small for in-home workout equipment. But I love running with my dog, Benny. He is a long-legged mutt who matches me stride for stride. What else can we do to exercise together outdoors safely?

Who needs expensive home equipment or a gym membership when you are lucky enough to have a canine workout buddy? The secret to improving your health may be just a tail wag away. Getting fit with your dog in organized, supervised workouts is gaining in interest and popularity. My friend Dawn Celapino is a certified fitness instructor who created one of the country's first such programs about 15 years ago in San Diego called Leash Your Fitness. There are now similar groups around the country that stage workout classes with people and their leashed dogs.

Before I moved to Dallas, I regularly attended Dawn's classes with the dogs I had then, Chipper and Cleo. During the hour, we would do sprints and stretches, and nimbly weave through obstacle courses. We even did some yoga moves, like the downward dog. By the end of class, everyone—including the dogs—was grinning from ear to ear.

Maintaining a regular fitness program with your dog delivers many dividends for both of you: improved health; greater flexibility and strength; reduced risk for arthritis, diabetes, and heart disease; and my favorite, spending less money on veterinary and doctor bills.

Before you lace up your sneakers and grab the leash, however, book appointments for both of you to receive complete physical examinations. Discuss

Breed Byte

Don't expect your basset hound to take laps in your pool. Their short, stubby legs can't keep their heavy, long bodies afloat.

workout options that are best for you and your dog. Keep in mind that an activity that may work for one dog may not work for another, even if they are the same breed. Dogs with pushed-up faces, such as bulldogs, do not tolerate the heat easily. Long-legged, slender-framed dogs, such as greyhounds, can cover distance more effortlessly than, say, a thick-legged basset hound.

Spend a few minutes doing warm-up stretches and helping your dog prepare his muscles, too. One way is to have him sit up and beg, then play bow (outstretched front legs, head down low, and rear end up in the air), roll over, and slowly go in a large circle. Start modestly with a 5-minute walk. Strive to increase the distance and pace to 30 minutes or longer. For longer walks, bring water so that both of you to stay hydrated.

Other workout options include swimming and hiking. Or you might try a more dog-focused activity like agility or canine musical freestyle. (See Canine Jocks Rule!, page 142, for more suggestions.) 🐾

Don't Overdo It

Be careful not to overexert your dog on walks and during activities. If your dog normally has been able to keep up with you on a walk or tends to pull out ahead, but now is walking beside you or even lagging a bit behind you, he may be asking to rest. If he displays any of the following signs, stop the activity and allow him to rest.

- Drooping tongue
- Rapid panting—an early sign of overheating
- Hesitation—taking a few extra seconds before retrieving a tossed ball
- Weight shifting—using different muscle groups to offset soreness
- Staggered walking
- Muscle tremors
- Limping—check footpads for cuts and bruises and legs for sprains or muscle pulls

Changing Lives,
PARTING WAYS

In my days as a daily newspaper reporter, I marveled at how my favorite metro editor could juggle so many things so well. She seemed to take everything in stride—from last-minute press conferences to staffers who called in sick to abrupt changes in page layouts. Her secret to success? Recognizing that life tosses all of us curveballs and that the only constant in life is *change*.

That mindset certainly holds true when it comes to our dogs. Many of us adopt puppies or young adult dogs with good intentions of keeping them for the rest of their lives. Or a dog might enter our lives unexpectedly, due to the death of a relative or the merger of pets in a marriage.

Sadly, life can interfere with our best intentions. Events like divorce, the birth of a baby, relocating for a job, or the onset of pet allergies can change our ability to provide a home for our pets. Sometimes our dogs develop chronic health issues, or behavior issues arise that seem impossible to cure. Or a natural disaster separates us from our beloved canines.

If our dogs do spend their entire lives with us, we must face that time we wish never would occur: parting ways with our canine friend because of their death or ours.

We can't stop change, and we can't live forever. But we do our best to prepare for the unexpected curveballs life hurls our way. This section offers you survival skills to handle two major upheavals—divorce and death—and every change in between.

A IS FOR ACHES AND ARTHRITIS

It seems like yesterday I was trying to tone down Corky's leaping, sprinting, and quick-turn maneuvering—especially inside my home. But she is nearing her 14th birthday and has developed arthritis in her spine. She takes time to stand up from a nap and to steady her legs, and she moves stiffly. What can I do to make her more comfortable?

It is hard to see our good old dogs walk gingerly, wince when standing up, or yip with pain. The percentage of dogs who develop arthritis is unknown, but this condition seems particularly common in large and long-backed breeds, as well as overweight dogs.

Two ways you can help relieve Corky's pain and mobility limitations are through exercise and diet. Keeping your dog engaged in daily exercise keeps her from turning into a sofa lounger. Rather than reducing exercise, it's time to modify Corky's routine. Transition to taking her on shorter, more frequent walks on level surfaces. If she's a ball chaser, roll one for her to fetch instead of tossing it.

As for diet, excessive adipose (fat) tissue not only packs on the pounds and impairs mobility but also secretes hormones that produce pain, especially in an arthritic dog. According to the Association for Pet Obesity Prevention, more than 50 percent of dogs in the

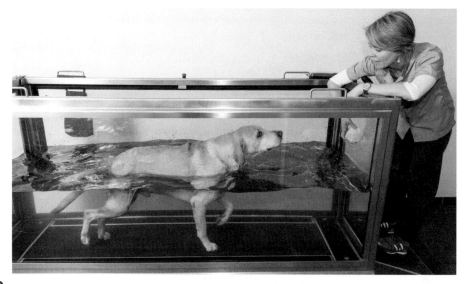

United States are overweight or obese. Even a few extra pounds can reduce a dog's life span, in some cases by as much as five years. Feeding Corky the right portions and not heaping on treats will help prevent her from transforming into a hairy ottoman.

Even if your dog is diagnosed with some form of arthritis such as hip dysplasia or osteoarthritis of the knee or other joint, consider these additional tactics to ease the aches and pains.

Think outside the (conventional) box. Look into acupuncture, therapeutic massage, hydrotherapy, and laser therapy sessions conducted by certified professionals. Hydrotherapy can ease aching joints with supervised swimming in pools as well as walking the dog on an underwater treadmill.

Fight the pain safely. Pain management medications prescribed by a veterinarian, such as anti-inflammatories and analgesics, can reduce swelling and pain in the joints, but steer clear of human medications such as acetaminophen (Tylenol) or ibuprofen (Advil), as they are both extremely toxic to dogs.

Make sure that Corky has regular veterinary checkups, and work with your veterinarian to find the best combination of pain management, diet, and exercise that will keep your companion comfortable in her old age. 🐾

TIPS FOR GOLDEN OLDIES

I was caught off guard the other day when I took a close look at my dog, Benji, and realized how gray his muzzle has become. It seems like just yesterday that he was a rambunctious puppy, but he is nearly 10. He pauses now before he gingerly jumps up on the sofa or on my bed, and he stops about 15 minutes into our daily neighborhood walks. How can I help Benji enjoy his golden years?

The graying of America has begun, and that applies to both people and dogs. One out of every three dogs—about 18 million—is 7 years or older. For most breeds, that equates to senior citizenship status. We get AARP cards at age 50; perhaps dogs should get AARF cards when they reach the equivalent milestone birthday!

Since Benji has been your faithful pal since his puppy days, he deserves a bit of pampering. One thing you should

189

Start by putting one hand on your dog's shoulder or side to comfort him, and use the other to pet him front to back with your palm. You can use more pressure if Benji is not in pain. For a dog with severe joint problems, gently stroke from the knee up to the hip and the mid-back to get that extra fluid out and reduce swelling.

You can also temporarily improve circulation in Benji's hips by warming a wet towel in the dryer for 10 to 15 minutes until it is just damp and placing it on his hips while he's resting.

The moisture in the towel retains heat better. This pampering works wonders on dogs of all ages. If you use an electric heating pad on your dog, do so at medium heat and for only 15 to 20 minutes. Stay with your dog to be sure the pad doesn't slip or he doesn't chew on the cord. If he seems uncomfortable, stop.

spend some money on is a checkup at the veterinary clinic. Two common reasons for aging dogs like Benji to require extra coaxing to get on or off furniture or in and out of cars are arthritis and hip dysplasia.

You also should rule out an acute injury. Please book a senior wellness appointment for Benji. This type of exam involves blood, urine, and stool samples that are studied by a veterinarian to gauge how Benji's kidneys, heart, and other key health aspects are functioning.

At home, treat Benji to regular therapeutic massages. Just 5 to 10 minutes a day can help maintain his muscle tone, range of motion in the joints, and comfort level. Practice a massage technique called *effleurage*, French for "light massage." It is petting with a purpose. Have Benji sit, stand, or lie down on his belly.

Look online for sales on sturdy pet ramps to help Benji get on and off the sofa. Or, if you are handy with tools, you can also create an inexpensive ramp using old carpet remnants or rugs and blocks of wood.

Pay attention to any signs of fading eyesight or hearing. Be sure to give him more frequent bathroom breaks, and keep tabs on the health of his teeth and gums in case he needs to switch to softer food. With loving care, I'm sure Benji will enjoy his last years in comfort. 🐾

A DOG'S LIFE

The old saying that one year in a dog's life equals seven human years is roughly true, but the following chart gives a more accurate comparison based on the dog's weight. Larger dogs generally have shorter lives than smaller ones. Of course, this is just a guideline—factors such as breed, lifestyle, and overall health are also important.

Age of dog	0–20 lbs.	20–50 lbs.	50–90 lbs.	>90 lbs.
5	36	37	40	42
6	40	42	45	49
7	44	47	50	56
8	48	51	55	64
9	52	56	61	71
10	56	60	66	78
11	60	65	72	86
12	64	69	77	93
13	68	74	82	101
14	72	78	88	108
15	76	83	93	115
16	80	87	99	123
17	84	92	104	
18	88	96	109	
19	92	101	115	
20	96	105	120	

■ = adult   ■ = senior   ■ = geriatric

Created by Fred Metzner, DVM, State College, Pennsylvania

191

DOGGY DEMENTIA

Zeke, my black-and-tan terrier mix, is 15. She used to love stalking squirrels, but now she would rather sleep all day. On walks, she can be only a few feet away from me but all of a sudden will start looking around and acting as if she has completely lost me. In the house, she sometimes stares blankly at the walls. Can dogs develop dementia in the way people do?

I am sorry to hear about Zeke. Memory loss and signs of confusion in older dogs may be symptoms of cognitive dysfunction syndrome, which is often described with the acronym DISH: disorientation, interaction reduction, sleep difficulties, and house soiling. Zeke is clearly disoriented, because she wanders aimlessly, becomes lost in your house, and stares blankly at walls. You may have noticed other changes in her behavior as well. Sleeping more during the day, waking up in the middle of the night, and barking for no apparent reason are also telltale signs. House soiling by a senior dog can be caused by forgetfulness but may be a sign of a medical problem.

In the past, owners—as well as many veterinarians—usually dismissed these symptoms as normal signs of aging. But today, growing gray in the muzzle doesn't have to automatically mean cognitive dysfunction. I encourage you to take Zeke for a thorough veterinary exam.

Older dogs need more frequent checkups, and many veterinarians recommend a senior wellness exam. This particular series of tests at age 7 (sooner for giant breeds) establishes a baseline of health and can uncover potentially serious problems before symptoms become unmanageable. Fortunately, treatments are now available that may not cure age-related canine dysfunction but can at least slow down the degenerative process.

In addition to a visit to your family veterinarian, you might consider consulting a veterinary specialist who can perform specific tests, such as ultrasound or MRI, to determine if there is a medical reason (age-related kidney or liver problems, for example) for changes in Zeke's behavior or if Zeke is displaying signs of cognitive dysfunction syndrome.

You can't put the brakes on the number of birthdays your dog has seen, but you can take steps to keep her feeling years younger. Veterinary researchers are learning ways to manage canine senility with memory-improving medications and specially formulated senior dog foods to ensure that a dog's final years are happy and healthy. There are several ways you can make Zeke's final years truly golden.

Before visiting your veterinarian, write down a list of all the symptoms you have noticed: for example, if Zeke seems to forget her name, fails to greet you when you come home, or wanders away from you in the middle of receiving affection. Take note of any changes in appetite, elimination habits, and physical condition.

Reinforce basic commands and add some new ones. You *can* teach an old dog new tricks, and doing so helps keep her mind alert and functioning. Teach her to sit before you head out the door for a walk or to shake paws before you set down her food bowl. (If her hearing is fading, you can teach her to look to you for hand signals.)

Keep your dog mentally stimulated by playing a game of hide-and-seek with food treats stashed in different rooms of the house. Or serve up interesting food puzzles, such as a hard rubber hollow toy filled with peanut butter.

Start going on shorter but more frequent walks, if possible. Regular exercise increases oxygen delivery to the brain, which can help your dog's mental abilities and keep her aging muscles working more smoothly. Stick to smooth surfaces that won't jar her joints. Vary the routes to expose her to new sights, sounds, and smells.

Encourage your dog to stretch. Prior to playtime or walks, have your dog get into a play bow position—head down, front legs low and stretched forward, and back end up. Lure your dog into this fun posture by lowering a treat under her nose. This natural full-body stretch helps improve circulation and warm the muscles. After a walk or activity, gently stretch your dog's legs and massage her torso.

Provide plenty of water. As dogs age, they tend to drink less and run the risk of dehydration. Add a few more water bowls around your home, and measure the water in the morning and at night to make sure your dog drinks enough water. Wipe up spills so that your dog doesn't slip and injure herself.

Unfortunately, our dogs don't live forever, but these measures can make Zeke's senior days better ones for the both of you. 🐾

TIME TO RETIRE?

Three times a week, I take Nugget, my certified therapy dog, to visit a nursing home and a children's cancer hospital. We spend an hour or two greeting the residents. Nugget has been a therapy dog for about eight years, and at age 10, she's a senior herself! Lately, I've noticed that she isn't as excited as she used to be when I put on her therapy vest, and she takes forever to get into the car. When she comes home from a therapy visit, she seems tired and even a bit sad. Why is she acting this way?

Therapy animals spread joy wherever they go. Animal-assisted programs can change and even save lives. It is just as important, however, that the therapy dogs' needs are met. Owners need to be on the lookout for signs of stress or burnout in their four-legged ambassadors of love. Therapy dogs are emotionally affected by sadness and pain in those they visit. They can get stressed and exhausted.

It takes two to make a good therapy team, and both must be committed to performing the task. It sounds as though you and Nugget have done a lot of good together, but even though you may still love the visits, you need to respect Nugget's wishes. She is showing signs that she is ready for retirement.

Therapy dogs who are ready to go home, or retire completely, will respond more slowly to cues. They will become more distracted on visits and may spend more time at the water bowl than working with the patients. Sometimes a dog will want to spend more time visiting one resident at the hospital instead of making the rounds.

Nugget, in her own sweet way, is letting you know that she is ready to spend more time in your home than in a nursing home or hospital. You need to honor her message. In some cases, retired therapy dogs happily take on a new role of serving as temperament test dogs for other dogs being tested for therapy work. Perhaps Nugget can usher in a new generation of therapy dogs in your city as a four-legged mentor.

Take Time to Help Others

If you have a well-mannered, obedient dog who enjoys meeting all types of people of all ages, you may have a dog who would enjoy making therapy visits. Although Labrador retrievers rank at the top in terms of the number of certified therapy dogs, dogs of any type can do this work if they have the right temperament.

I have been blessed to have not one but two therapy dogs: my late, great Chipper, a husky mix, and now, Kona, my terrier mix. Together, we have visited people in memory care centers, hospitals, nursing homes, elementary schools, and kid camps at animal shelters. It has been one of my favorite ways to give back.

Therapy dogs need a thorough grounding in obedience training. They must be able to sit patiently by a wheelchair or hospital bed. They must be able to tolerate a lot of noise and distractions without fear. They must accept having their ears pulled and their tails yanked by people without reacting aggressively. Many therapy dogs learn to gently place a paw on a lap or to nudge a patient's hand to encourage interaction.

Equally important to the success of a good therapy team is the person holding the other end of the leash. Human volunteers should have good dog sense, a desire to bring cheer to others, and a willingness to follow guidelines set by the facility they are visiting.

The requirements to become a therapy dog are outlined on the websites of such national organizations as Love on a Leash and Pet Partners.

HOW PETS EXPRESS GRIEF

Our dogs, Bosco and Bubba, and our cat, Clyde, were inseparable buddies. We often remarked how lucky we were never to have to deal with jealousy issues among our loving trio. Bubba, our fun-loving bullmastiff, recently became very ill, and we asked our veterinarian to come to the house to euthanize him. We did this in the presence of Bosco and Clyde.

Now the two of them seem so sad all the time. They eat a little, but don't beg for food, and Bosco is usually a chowhound. Are dogs and cats capable of grieving the loss of another pet?

Your four-legged trio clearly loved one another. Please accept heart-filled hugs and wags from me and my own canine pack. Just as we do, dogs form strong emotional bonds to chosen people and other animals, and they feel a wide range of emotions, including grief. Dogs are also big fans of predictability. They like household routines. Not all dogs handle changes in the household as well as others.

Psychologists and veterinary behaviorists confirm what pet parents already know: Dogs and cats do experience loss and sadness. In two surveys—one by the ASPCA and one by the New Zealand Companion Animal Council—researchers surveyed pet parents and asked them how the surviving pets in their families responded to the departure of a four-legged companion. Among their findings:

- 60 percent of dogs continually sniffed and searched the spot in the home where the departed pet usually napped.

- 61 percent of dogs became more clingy and needy with their pet parents.

- 27 percent of dogs began whining and whimpering after the pet was gone.

- About one-third of dogs ate less and slept more in the days following the death of an animal friend.

- 66 percent displayed four or more behavior changes after the death of a dog or cat companion.

The conclusion: Surviving pets do suffer some degree of stress when a beloved four-legged companion dies.

You did a wonderful thing by including Bosco and Clyde in this farewell act for Bubba. Whenever possible, allow other household pets to sniff and inspect the body of the dead pet.

Although there is no scientific evidence to support the notion that checking the body will help the surviving pets to cope emotionally, at least it lets them know for sure what has happened and, at best, may help bring closure.

To help Bosco and Clyde cope with the loss of Bubba, introduce them to new toys, entice them to play a favorite game, and offer high-value treats. Spend more time giving them affection. If their grief-related behaviors persist, please consult your veterinarian about temporarily giving them medication to cope with their depression or anxieties.

Don't rush to bring home a new dog or cat, thinking that this newcomer will help ease their grief. Some people are so overcome by their own grief during this "rebound" period that they choose an inappropriate replacement pet. Introducing a new pet too soon may add to the sadness and confusion the survivors are feeling. Just like you, Bosco and Clyde need time to properly grieve the loss of Bubba. 🐾

KNOWING WHEN TO SAY GOODBYE

My feisty, friendly dog, Sparky, is a 7-year-old Chihuahua who has been diagnosed with bone cancer in his front leg. I know that even if we beat this cancer, I will eventually have to make the painful decision to euthanize him so he doesn't suffer, either from illness or old age. How will I know when that time has arrived?

Saying goodbye to a loyal pet is one of life's hardest decisions. If your dog becomes terminally ill or is critically injured, or the cost of treatment is beyond your means, euthanasia may be a valid option. Fortunately for Sparky, canine medicine has made amazing strides in treating cancer and other serious diseases. Cancer centers for companion animals now exist throughout the country.

Bone cancer is serious, however, and it is good to ask this question before it reaches the point where you don't have the time to carefully consider all options. The more you are able to prepare for the possible loss of your pet, the fewer regrets you will have.

There is a growing trend for veterinarians to specialize in pet hospice care and at-home euthanasia. Lap of Love Veterinary Hospice, started in 2009 in Florida by a pair of veterinarians named Mary Gardner and Dani McVety, now has dozens of centers all over the country.

Modeled after hospice for people, veterinary hospice is not about extending suffering, but rather preventing suffering from occurring at all. The practice takes a team approach that involves the family and the veterinary staff working together to maintain comfort and quality of life for terminally ill or geriatric pets until natural death happens or the family chooses euthanasia. Veterinary hospice focuses on comforting the pet, not finding a cure for a terminal disease.

Before Sparky becomes seriously ill, check out Lap of Love and also talk with your veterinarian about what is involved in euthanasia. You may be amazed at how peaceful and pain-free this procedure is. Preparing for euthanasia includes determining when and where the procedure should take place. Your veterinarian might make a house call.

You will need to decide if you want your pet's body to be buried or cremated. Think about your own needs and determine if you would prefer to be alone after the procedure or if you want to spend time with a special friend.

When is the right time? That is certainly an individual call, but quality of life is your guidepost in making the decision. You will probably know when it is right by paying careful attention to Sparky's signals. He may stop eating, be unable to go to the bathroom on his own, and begin to sleep all the time. Look for signs of pain or discomfort that cannot be eased with medication.

Please keep this final thought in mind: The very definition of euthanasia, from the Greek *eu* (good) and *thanatos* (death), means the end of physical suffering for our animal friends. It is truly the last gift we can give them. 🐾

Breed Byte

Named for the region of Mexico where it was first discovered in the mid-nineteenth century, the Chihuahua stands short on stature but long on longevity. On average, this breed lives 18 to 20 years.

How Will I Know It Is the Right Time?

Lap of Love veterinarians say end of life depends on the pet. They offer this checklist to help pet parents know when it is the right time for euthanasia.

- ☐ Is no longer interested in food or water

- ☐ Has chronic incontinence (accidents in the house) or is unable to go to the bathroom without assistance

- ☐ No longer greets you when you come home

- ☐ No longer patrols the yard or protects their territory

- ☐ Has stopped grooming

- ☐ No longer wags his/her tail, or holds it down all the time

- ☐ Isolates from the people or other pets in the home, particularly in unusual places

- ☐ Is not interested in playing or doing other favorite things

- ☐ Is unable to stand or walk independently

- ☐ Shows a change in attitude (depression, aggression, confusion)

- ☐ Has fewer "good" days than bad

INHERITING A PAMPERED POOCH

My grandmother recently died, leaving behind a 4-year-old papillon named Sugar, who was a wonderful companion to her. Grandma doted on this dog, serving her food on china plates, dressing her up with pink ribbons, and letting her sit in her own dining room chair. She was also practical and discussed with me in advance how to care for Sugar after she died.

I love this little dog, but it is clear that she misses my grandmother a lot. What can I do to help Sugar understand that she has a new loving home?

Your grandmother showed good sense in making sure that her sweet dog had a good home after she died. You may not treat Sugar with quite the same level of devotion, but you can take steps to introduce your own style of pampering.

Our pets can't tell us in words how they feel when a beloved person leaves them, but they do display signs of mourning. Some dogs show amazing dedication to their deceased owners, so be aware that Sugar may show signs of stress and anxiety as she adjusts to her new life with you. Sugar may urinate in your house when you're not around, not eat much, excessively lick her paws, or go overboard to greet you each time you come home.

These behaviors can last days or weeks. Please consult your veterinarian concerning behavioral issues that affect your dog's health, especially lack of appetite.

Help Sugar adjust to your home by letting her sleep in your bedroom at night. Dogs are den creatures, and this will give her some comfort and a feeling of security. Offer her healthy outlets by

Breed Byte

Papillon is the French word for "butterfly." This fluffy toy breed is named for its large ears, which look like butterfly wings.

walking her daily, engaging her in games like fetch, and keeping the television or radio on when you're not at home to provide some welcome human noise. Invite some dog-friendly friends over to dote on Sugar and improve her mood.

You cannot replace your grandmother in the eyes of Sugar, but you do have a wonderful opportunity to form a new friendship with her and to provide her with a loving and stable home that honors your grandmother's memory. 🐾

Faithful Fidos

A famous story that illustrates the devotion of dogs involves a terrier named Bobby who lived in Edinburgh, Scotland, in the mid-1800s. When his owner died, Bobby attended the graveside service and then lay on the grave every night for the next 14 years until his own death. Members of the town were so moved by this canine devotion that they erected a statue and water fountain in Bobby's memory that stands to this day.

Then there was Hachiko, the faithful dog of Japan. Every afternoon, this Akita would wait at the Shibuya train station for his owner, Eizaburo Ueno, a university professor in Tokyo, to return from work. Ueno died at his office of a cerebral hemorrhage in 1925, but for nine years, Hachiko waited at the train station every day in all types of weather. This loyal dog is also commemorated with a statue in his honor.

EXERCISING WILL POWER

I share my town home with a cocker spaniel, a pug, and two cats. I hope to be around to provide for them to the end, but I know that I should have a plan in writing on how to care for them in case I die first. They love each other, and I want to be sure they are never separated or taken to an animal shelter. What kind of legal protection do I have to ensure that my wishes are carried out if I should die before my pets?

Sadly, about 500,000 pets each year are surrendered to animal shelters in the United States because their people became too ill to care for them, had to move into a nursing home, or died unexpectedly.

In the chaos, trauma, and upheaval that often occurs when someone dies, pets can easily get overlooked while funeral arrangements are being made. Prearranging the care of your pets gives you peace of mind, and it's never too early to draw up a will, a living trust, or some other legal document to specify how your pets should be cared for.

Legally, pets are considered to be personal property, which means you have a right to determine what happens to them in the event of your death. You are absolutely right that any arrangements should be made in writing, because verbal agreements cannot be legally enforced.

Amy Shever is the founder and executive director of 2nd Chance 4 Pets, a nonprofit group on a mission to educate people who want to plan ahead for their pets' ongoing care. She recommends these three steps:

○ Identify caregivers who would be willing to care for your pets in the hours, days, or weeks after an emergency. Identify those willing to adopt your pets should you die, and get their consent in writing.

○ Write out your instructions on how your pets should be cared for as well as detailing any special type of care. File this information with your will and other important papers.

○ Create a pet fund. Set aside funds each month to cover the temporary or permanent cost to care for your pets. Be sure to budget in their food, veterinary care, and supplies.

Keep a card in your wallet that specifies who should be contacted to take care of your pets in the event of an emergency. Include their phone numbers. Post this information on the front of your refrigerator or in another highly visible place in your home. Give a copy to your veterinarian and one to your chosen caretaker.

Contact your county or state bar association for names of attorneys who practice estate planning and animal law. Recognize the difference between wills and trusts. Essentially, a will directs who gets what after a person dies. A trust can be implemented while you're still alive (should you no longer be able to care for your pet). Both can be changed should you want to do so.

There are many types of trusts, and the rules vary from state to state. With an honorary trust, for example, you can declare one person as trustee to be in charge of the money paid out for the care of your pets and another person in charge of the actual care of your pets. This can establish some checks and balances.

If you do not have a friend or family member willing to care for your pets, look into pet retirement homes, sanctuaries, or shelters that accept pets as permanent residents after an owner's death. Consult with your veterinarian or an animal behaviorist about a reputable shelter or animal organization you can designate to care for your pet. Ask for references and a written agreement that spells out your wishes.

You can also name a shelter, veterinary hospital, or other animal agency as your beneficiary. In exchange for agreeing to be your pets' caretaker,

you bequeath them your home or other asset.

Providing legal protection for pets is a growing area of the law. As much as we do not want to think about dying, it is important to determine who will take care of the pets we leave behind. These steps can ease your worries and provide a healthy, happy future for your pets. 🐾

203

WHO GETS THE DOG?

My husband and I are calling it quits after 10 years of marriage. We don't have children, but we do have a wonderful boxer who loves both of us. With his energy and ready grin, Ali has brought us much joy. Our breakup has been fairly amicable, and we have agreed on who gets what, with the exception of Ali. We both want him. We are thinking about joint custody, but would that be best for Ali's emotional well-being?

With about 40 percent of marriages ending in divorce, more and more dogs are getting caught in an emotional tug-of-war between dueling spouses. When couples feud, the yelling, slamming doors, and icy silences can take an emotional and physical toll on their ever-loyal dogs. Just like kids, dogs can actually become physically ill because of the heightened level of stress in the house. Behavioral problems may develop, such as separation anxiety or aggression.

Divorce often brings out the worst in people, and emotions run high. Dogs sometimes become pawns in divorce settlements, and they can become the real victims. I've heard of cases in which one spouse would not let the other spouse see the dog, while using visitation privileges for leverage for a final settlement deal. But it doesn't have to be that way. Like you, many couples work out an amicable agreement to share custody rather than use the dog as a weapon.

To maintain a sense of normalcy for your dog, stick to your routines as much as possible. Dogs are creatures of habit and look forward to regular activities, such as the Saturday trip to the dog park or their morning game of tug-of-war. They are adaptable, though, and can certainly adjust to the routines in two separate households.

Let me share the story of a couple who successfully kept their dog in mind during their divorce. This East Coast couple regarded their yellow Lab, Beau, as their four-legged kid, and neither wanted to be without him. During their separation and ultimate divorce, Beau was the only topic the couple did not fight about. Neither wanted the dog to feel torn loyalties, so they worked out an informal custody arrangement in which Beau would switch households every six weeks to three months.

The two now live about 250 miles apart, so they meet halfway to transfer Beau from one car to the other. Although he initially displayed confusion and sadness by barking and constantly seeking attention, Beau is always delighted to see the other person and has learned that he can be secure in two different places.

Sticking to familiar rituals is vital. When Beau is with the ex-husband, the two enjoy long, daily walks. When Beau stays with the ex-wife, they play a favorite game called Shoe for a Chew. The rules are simple: Beau retrieves a shoe from the closet in exchange for a chew treat. During his absence, each owner occasionally sends Beau a small toy or treat with his or her scent on it, and they talk to him on the phone once in a while.

Beau sniffs attentively when he receives a toy, card, or treat in the mail from one of his pet parents. Several years after the divorce, he happily moves between his households without signs of stress or anxiety. 🐾

BANISH THE PACKING BOX BLUES

My wife and I have grown tired of the cold winters in Minneapolis. Our house is too big for us now that our children are grown, so we are retiring and moving to a condo in Palm Springs, California. Maggie, our springer spaniel mix, is sweet, but she gets nervous whenever there is a change in the daily routine. How can we help her stay calm when she sees packing boxes all over the house and, even worse, movers coming through the front door?

Moving is one of life's big stressors for both dogs and people. The break in the routine—with furniture being moved, items being packed, and strangers coming in and out of the house—can take a toll on a dog's self-confidence and feeling of security. Fortunately, dogs tend to bond more with their people than with their zip codes. The good news for Maggie is that once she settles into the new locale, she will happily continue her great life with the two of you.

While you are in the process of packing your belongings and preparing the house for sale, maintain Maggie's usual routine as much as possible, especially your daily walks—the exercise will help all of you unleash some tension and stress. Speak to her in an upbeat, happy voice to reassure her. Help her feel more comfortable with the changing household by setting up cardboard boxes in rooms all over your house. As you pack items, let Maggie sniff and explore.

Point out the box to her, say the word *box*, and then hand her a treat. You are building up a positive association between the boxes and the treats for Maggie. Take a break once in a while and pay special attention to her by reinforcing her basic obedience commands or having her perform one of her favorite tricks for treats.

On moving day, take Maggie to visit a favorite friend's home or to a doggy day care if she is already a regular there. The doggy day care provides a perfect outlet for her to unleash her energy with canine chums in a safe, supervised setting. When you pick her up at the end of the day, she will be tired and relaxed, even when walking into a near-empty house.

If you do opt to keep her at home, choose a room that has already been cleared of all furnishings. Place a big sign on colored paper on the door to alert the movers that your dog is inside. During the hustle of moving items, you don't want to risk Maggie escaping in fright and getting lost or hit by a car. If she likes her crate, let her stay in there

with her favorite chew toy and water in a closed room.

If she doesn't have a crate, provide her with her familiar bedding, a couple of favorite toys, a chew toy, and water. Turn on a sound machine or a portable radio to mute the sounds of the moving crew. Make sure she is wearing a collar and ID tag with her name and your cell phone number. She should also have a microchip ID.

It is very important that you take her for at least a 10-minute walk every few hours. Make sure you put her leash on before you leave the room. Encourage her to meet and greet the movers if they are willing. Speak in happy and calm

tones. Dogs are masters at picking up our emotions.

Before you move into your new condo, see if your real estate agent is willing to place one of your used T-shirts or towels and a couple of Maggie's saliva-slobbered toys inside the condo before you arrive. Just mail them in advance of your cross-country trek. That way, when Maggie first steps into your new place, she will immediately smell and see familiar objects that will help her feel more at home. 🐾

TRAINING TIPS

Teaching **Watch me**

Before you can teach a dog anything, you have to have his attention. Teaching this cue will help all the rest of your training and will improve your dog's focus on you rather than distractions at home or when you are out and about together.

1 Hold a treat in your hand to get your dog's attention. You may need to wave it front of his nose, but most dogs will be watching you eagerly.

2 Keeping your eyes on your dog's face, say *Watch me* as you slowly bring the treat near your eye.

3 As soon as your dog locks eyes with you, quickly say *Good watch me!* and hand over the treat.

4 After he has aced this a few times in a row, make him wait a couple of seconds before rewarding him. This keeps his focus on you and makes him realize he needs to pay attention in order to get the treat.

Teaching **Sit**

When a dog is sitting, she can't get into trouble. This is one of the most important cues to teach your dog. Resist trying to push down on her rump—she may think you're trying to play, or she may feel nervous and try to get away.

1 Position yourself facing your dog.

2 Hold a treat in front of her nose.

3 Say *Sit* as you slowly lift the treat above her head.

4 Let gravity do its job. As your dog moves her head up to follow the treat, her rump will sink to the floor. Immediately say *Good sit!* and hand over the treat.

5 Once your dog is sitting promptly at your cue, start making her wait a few seconds before rewarding her.

Teaching **Stay**

The goal of this cue is to teach your dog to wait patiently while you do something else. Start by asking for just a few seconds of holding the position, then gradually increase the amount of time. After your dog learns to stay while leashed, practice for a while without holding on to the leash, then move on to practicing with no leash.

1 Leash your dog, place her at your side, and say *Sit*.

2 Toss a treat or two in front of her but just out of her reach. Say *Stay*.

3 If she pulls for the treat, don't say anything. Be calm and hold on to the leash. Only reward her when she stops pulling and stays in place.

4 Once she holds her position for even a few seconds, say *Good stay* and then *Okay* as you loosen the leash so she can get the treat.

5 When she stays while eyeing a treat in front of her, keep hold of the leash as you say *Stay* and toss another treat about two feet in front of her.

6 When she stops trying to reach the treat, say *Good stay*, then *Okay* as you loosen the leash so she can retrieve her reward. When she has learned to *Sit* and *Stay*, practice *Stay* from the down position.

Teaching **Come**

It's important to train this cue in stages, starting in a quiet, confined area and slowly moving to larger spaces with more distractions. Start your sessions with a 12- to 20-foot leash or clothesline that can be safely tethered to your dog's collar or harness. Work on refining your recall off leash in a confined area until you are very confident that your dog will return when called.

1 Cue your dog to *Sit* and *Stay* while facing you. Slowly walk backward about five feet from him as you hold on to the leash.

2 In an enthusiastic tone, say your dog's name and *Come!* Bend forward to encourage him, but don't repeat the command.

3 When he reaches you, say *Good come!* and hand him a treat. Practice in short sessions until he understands that *Come* means to head right to you.

4 Once he'll come consistently from a *Stay* position, practice calling him from farther away.

5 The next step is to let him wander away from you, still on the leash, before you call him. If he isn't paying attention, you can give a gentle tug on the leash as you call him. Eventually you can drop the leash while he drags it (so you can grab it if you need to) and then progress to practicing off leash.

Teaching **Find your spot**

This cue tells your dog it's time to head for her bed or blanket, lie down, and chill. When we're traveling and teaching class, Kona knows *Find your spot* means she can relax and be off duty for a while. Your dog needs to know how to *Stay* before you can teach this cue.

1 Practice near your dog's bed or a favorite blanket folded on the floor. Stand two or three feet from the bed with your dog sitting beside you. Toss a treat onto the bed. Say *Find your spot* as you point to the bed to encourage your dog to go toward it.

2 Let her eat the treat, then have her sit or lie down on the bed. After a few seconds, say *Good spot!* as you give her another treat to reinforce the desired behavior.

3 Practice until your dog associates the tossed treat with your pointing toward the bed. Then instead of tossing the treat, point at the bed as you give the cue. Wait to reward her until she is on the bed.

4 Once she is doing that consistently, tell her to *Stay*. Gradually extend the amount of time you expect her to stay on the bed before you reward her.

Teaching **Off**

A dog who jumps up on people is displaying bad manners. Your friends and family will appreciate being greeted politely by your dog without being knocked over. Instead of yelling at him, the trick is to teach your dog to do something else, like sit. You'll need a long leash (at least six feet) and a helper.

1 Attach the leash to your dog's collar or harness. Stand behind your dog, holding the leash in your hand. Have your helper approach your dog from the front, without trying to pet him.

2 As soon as your dog starts to jump up toward the person, say *Off!* and quickly pull the leash straight down and to the side. The goal is to stop your dog from moving forward and up.

3 The second your dog has all four paws on the floor, tell him to *Sit* and reward him right away when he does. Make him wait until the person approaches him to give a greeting.

In time, your dog will learn that he scores no attention from the visitor and no treats when he leaps up, but he is rewarded with pats and treats when he sits politely to greet people.

USEFUL WEBSITES

2nd Chance 4 Pets
www.2ndchance4pets.org

The Acorn Project (for deaf dogs)
www.acorn-project.org

The American Herding Breed Association
www.ahba-herding.org

American Kennel Club
www.akc.org

American Sighthound Field Association
www.asfa.org

American Society for the Prevention of Cruelty to Animals
www.aspca.org

American Veterinary Medical Association
www.avma.org

Ashley Whippet Invitational
www.ashleywhippet.com

The Association of Professional Dog Trainers
https://apdt.com

Canine Freestyle Federation
https://canine-freestyle.org

Canine Learning Centers
www.k9lrng.com

CT Dog Gone Recovery Volunteers
www.ctdgrv.org

Deaf Dog Education Action Fund
www.deafdogs.org

DOGTV
www.dogtv.com

Dogster
www.dogster.com

Fear Free
https://fearfreepets.com

FIDO Friendly Magazine
www.fidofriendly.com

Lost Dogs of America
www.lostdogsofamerica.org

Love on a Leash
https://loveonaleash.org

Mobile RVing
www.mobilerving.com

National Association of Canine Scent Work
www.nacsw.net

The North American Dog Agility Council
www.nadac.com

North American Flyball Association
www.flyball.org

North America Diving Dogs
https://northamericadivingdogs.com

National Association of Professional Pet Sitters
www.petsitters.org

Pet First Aid 4U
www.petfirstaid4u.com

Pet Life Radio
www.petliferadio.com

Pet Partners
https://petpartners.org

Pet Sitters International
www.petsit.com

Preventive Vet
www.preventivevet.com

Pro Pet Hero
www.catanddogfirstaid.com

Skyhoundz
www.skyhoundz.com

UFO World Cup Frisbee Dog Series
www.ufoworldcup.org

US Disc Dog Nationals
https://usddn.com

United States Dog Agility Association
www.usdaa.com

What a Great Dog Training Center
www.whatagreatdog.com

World Canine Freestyle Organization
www.worldcaninefreestyle.org

RECOMMENDED READING

The Big Book of Tricks for the Best Dog Ever by Larry Kay and Chris Perondi, Workman Publishing, 2019

Careers with Dogs by Kim Campbell Thornton, CompanionHouse Books, 2011

Fit Dog: Tips and Tricks to Give Your Pet a Longer, Healthier, Happier Life by Arden Moore, Firefly Books, 2015

From Fearful to Fear Free by Marty Becker, Lisa Radosta, Wailani Sung, and Mikkel Becker, Health Communications, Inc., 2018

A Kid's Guide to Dogs by Arden Moore, Storey Publishing, 2020

Lucky Dog Lessons by Brandon McMillan, HarperOne, 2016

National Geographic Complete Guide to Pet Health, Behavior and Happiness by Gary Weitzman, DVM, National Geographic, 2019

What Dogs Want: A Visual Guide to Understanding Your Dog's Every Move, by Arden Moore, Firefly Books, 2012

ACKNOWLEDGMENTS

I give a big paws-up to all the animal behaviorists, veterinarians, and professional dog trainers who have guided me for the past two decades of learning all things d-o-g. Special thanks go to Cara Armour, Dr. Marty Becker, Dr. Debora Charles, Laura Christiansen, Erin Fenstermaker, Dr. Alice Moon-Fanelli, Larry Kay, Brandon McMillan, Maureen Patin, and Dr. Mike LoSasso.

I also unleash gratitude and appreciation to Lisa Hiley, my main editor, and the entire Storey Publishing team, who have believed in me since they published my first pet book more than 20 years ago.

INTERIOR PHOTO CREDITS

© absolutimages/stock.adobe.com, 177; © Alexandr/stock.adobe.com, 168; © Alexey Kuznetsov/stock.adobe.com, 17; © Alphotographic/iStock.com, 75; © annette shaff/stock.adobe.com, 23 and throughout; © antoine-photographe/stock.adobe.com, 189; © AS Photo Project/stock.adobe.com, 152; Courtesy of Atali Samuel Photography, 9; © BenAkiba/iStock.com, 138; © blinova/stock.adobe.com, 108; © Bob and Pam Langrish KA9Photo/Alamy Stock Photo, 62; © Budimir Jevtic/stock.adobe.com, 203; © ccestep8/stock.adobe.com, 211; © Chalabala/stock.adobe.com, 99; © corners74/stock.adobe.com, 195; © Crystal Madsen/stock.adobe.com, 81; © Csanad Kiss/Shutterstock.com, 12; © cynoclub/stock.adobe.com, 20, 50, 64; © DalaiFood/stock.adobe.com, 26; © daylight917/stock.adobe.com, 22; © DenisNata/stock.adobe.com, 60 l.; © Denny/stock.adobe.com, 142 l.; © deviddo/stock.adobe.com, 91; © dionoanomalia/stock.adobe.com, 169, 200; © DoraZett/stock.adobe.com, 39; © Douglas Pitcher/Shutterstock.com, 204; © Elayne/stock.adobe.com, 127; © Elles Rijsdijk/stock.adobe.com, 159; © encierro/stock.adobe.com, 120, 209; © Elisaveta Ivanova/iStock.com, 52; © Erik Lam/stock.adobe.com, 140; © EyeEm/Alamy Stock Photo, 78; Courtesy of Fear Free, LLC, 116; © feeferlump/stock.adobe.com, 143; © Fly_dragonfly/stock.adobe.com, 111; © fotowebbox/stock.adobe.com, 37; © freemixer/iStock.com, 135; © GlobalP/iStock.com, 157; © Golden Pixels LLC/Shutterstock.com, 155; © Guy Sagi/stock.adobe.com, 87; © Happy monkey/stock.adobe.com, 69; © hedgehog94/stock.adobe.com, 38; © hnijjar007/iStock.com, 112; © iagodina/stock.adoe.com, 151; © Inna Skaldutska/iStock.com, 71; © Inti St. Clair/stock.adobe.com, 103; © Iryna Khabliuk/Alamy Stock Photo, 212; © James Boardman/Alamy Stock Photo, 117; © Jason/stock.adobe.com, 40; © Javier brosch/stock.adobe.com, 94; © Jekatarinka/Shutterstock.com, 14 b. and throughout; © jenngarcia/stock.adobe.com, 14 t.; © jfjacobsz/stock.adobe.com, 93, 146; © johncan/Shutterstock.com, 45; © Julia/stock.adobe.com, 44; © Julia Bond/Shutterstock.com, 84; © julia_siomuha/stock.adobe.com, 54; © Julija/iStock.com, 197; © Justyna/stock.adobe.com, 160, 183; © Karoline Thalhofer/stock.adobe.com, 96, 126, 193; © Kathy images/stock.adobe.com, 207; © keira01/123RF.com, 46; © Kira-Yan/iStock.com, 18; © kisscsanad/stock.adobe.com, 47; © ksuksa/stock.adobe.com, 16, 142 r.; © Lambros Kazanas/Alamy Stock Photo, 5 ; © Lilia Solonari/Shutterstock.com, 82; © Lisa H/stock.adobe.com, 190; © Luka Tambaca/Alamy Stock Photo, 1; © Lunja/Shutterstock.com, 66; © Lutsiv Maxim/Shutterstock.com, 76; © MakroBetz/Depositphotos.com, 208; © martincp/stock.adobe.com, 61 r.; Mars Vilaubi © Storey Publishing, LLC, 133, 213; © Mary Swift/stock.adobe.com, 61 l., 181; © moodboard/stock.adobe.com, 178; © New Africa/Shutterstock.com, 43; © nicholas_dale/iStock.com, 100; © Noric_JPN/stock.adobe.com, 25; © pagan Mckenzie/Stocksy/stock.adobe.com, 74; © Petra Wegner/Alamy Stock Photo, 170; © Photoboyko/stock.adobe.com, 175; Pilleybianchi/Wikimedia/CC BY-SA 4.0, 57; © Pixel-Shot/stock.adobe.com, 172; © PLIX/stock.adobe.com, 2; © Prostock-Studio/iStock.com, 144; © Przemyslaw Iciak/stock.adobe.com, 136, 199; © psychoshadow/stock.adobe.com, 216; © Rawpixel.com/stock.adobe.com, 118; © Rixie/stock.adobe.com, 201; © Ryan/stock.adobe.com, 90; © SAJ/stock.adobe.com, 10; © SasaStock/stock.adobe.com, 123; © Sergio Victor Vega/ADDICTIVE STOCK/stock.adobe.com, 164; © serhiibobyk/stock.adobe.com, 210; © seroma72/123RF.com, 131; © skivi08/stock.adobe.com, 51; © Soloviova Liudmyla/stock.adobe.com, 147; © Sonja/stock.adobe.com, 28; © sopradit/stock.adobe.com, 129; © Stanley/Stockimo/Alamy Stock Photo, 106; © Stephen Flint/Alamy Stock Photo, 73; © sue/stock.adobe.com, 60 r.; © Svetlana Radayeva/stock.adobe.com, 198; © svetography/stock.adobe.com, 31 b.; © Tanya/stock.adobe.com, 32; © Tegan/stock.adobe.com, 114; © Thirawatana/stock.adobe.com, 29; © Timothy/stock.adobe.com, 104; © VeaVea/Stocksy/stock.adobe.com, 98; © vivienstock/stock.adobe.com, 184; © WavebreakMediaMicro/stock.adobe.com, 88; © Westend61 GmbH/Alamy Stock Photo, 186; © willbrasil21/stock.adobe.com, 34; © Wirestock/stock.adobe.com, 31 t.; © wonderlandstock/Alamy Stock Photo, 162; © xkunclova/Shutterstock.com, 48; © (Yulia Zavalishina) Юлия Завалишина/stock.adobe.com, 149

INDEX

Page numbers in **bold** indicate charts.

Love Your Pets
with More Books by Arden Moore

A Kid's Guide to Dogs
Learn all about breeds, body language, training, health care, and make-them-yourself dog treats and toys!

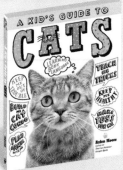

A Kid's Guide to Cats
Learn everything you want to know about your kitty friends, from what makes them tick to how to keep them healthy, with plenty of fun along the way.

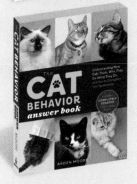

The Cat Behavior Answer Book, 2nd Edition
The browsable Q&A format offers practical advice and workable solutions to common problems.

Join the conversation. Share your experience with this book, learn more about Storey Publishing's authors, and read original essays and book excerpts at storey.com. Look for our books wherever quality books are sold or call 800-441-5700.